ONCE UPON A TIME IN BRADFORD

The chronicles of a
below average individual

SHAFEEQ YOUSSAF

First Published in Great Britain in 2021

Copyright © 2021 Shafeeq Youssaf

Fourth edition 2022

A CIP catalogue record for this book is available from the British Library

Cover Design by Creative Covers

Typesetting by Book Polishers

THE STANDARD OPENING CHAPTER WHERE I DESCRIBE MY TRAUMATIC AND IMPOVERISHED CHILDHOOD.

Let me start by saying, I've no idea who you are either. Now that we've got the introductions out of the way, it's time for the obvious disclaimer. This is quite possibly the most poorly written and pointless book ever published. If you carry on reading beyond this point, you've only got yourself to blame. If you're stupid enough to have actually paid for it, I also have some magic beans for sale that will provide you with riches beyond your wildest dreams.

Even though my declaration about the poor quality of the book is correct, you still have my blood, sweat, tears and the finest brain matter I have to offer in your mortal hands right now. This isn't because someone bashed me over the skull with this book (or an electronic device for the online version), although there is still time. You're probably my only reader, and that's almost certainly because you acquired it after clicking on the wrong button on the Amazon app. There's a decent chance you haven't even read it beyond the first few lines and utilised it to prop up that wobbly chair you've been vowing to fix for years. If you've slipped off the chair, kicked your legs in the air, and howled loudly, it won't be due to my jokes but more likely because you failed to wedge in my book firmly enough. Your Amazon review will reflect this and will read something like, "Ordered by mistake but was exactly what I had been seeking for years. Perfect length, height, and weight. It's part of the furniture now."

If you were expecting any rousing, tear-inducing, heart-wrenching speeches or any emotional resonance, you'd be advised to slap yourself. You won't get any tosh, like seize the day or live for the moment from me. What you will get are lame jokes, dubious philosophical claims, and uninteresting anecdotes. This won't appeal to modern readers, with their low boredom thresholds and limited attention spans.

The complete autonomy of self-publishing allows me to write whatever I want because I don't have any professional obligations to a publisher or any desire for validation. My writing is for personal amusement and possibly for the former professional football player, Des Walker. I'll talk more about that later. It could also serve as a history of my family for future generations.

The only things I had to offer for such a gargantuan undertaking were my inherent laziness, a complete absence of talent, and a propensity for serious stupidity.

If an opportunity knocked on my door, I'd grumble about the noise, explain it had the wrong door, and ask it not to disturb me again. Instead of "get up and go," I have "lay down and put your feet up." When I perish, my gravestone will read, "He blobbed in life, as expected." My time on this earth has been about as meaningful as an apostrophe in a plural.

As I started writing, I declared my intentions to my wife. She described it as a colossal waste of time and enquired if I was having a mid-life crisis. Mid-life resurrection was my more apt description. Coincidentally, this was the point where she had stopped reading an early draft. Her disparaging review and the lack of interest gave me licence to be less than flattering about her from this point onwards. I wish she had read more of it because she would have been the perfect proof-reader. Who else, on God's clean earth, was more experienced at detecting and magnifying my mistakes?

When she discovered some of the book would be about my childhood hero, Des Walker, she claimed it mirrored Stephen King's horror novel, *Misery*, which was subsequently made into a successful film. That story revolved around a writer who was held captive by his biggest fan. This fan was a serial killer, and any parallels between the two books are purely coincidental.

This would be the perfect time for some introspective and contemplative music in the background. The music, which accurately encapsulates this part of the book, would be Kevin MacLeod's 'Long Road Ahead.' One of the reasons I'd recommend this particular music is because the long literary road ahead will be bumpy and unbelievably juggled. It will flow like a well-cooked jelly. There are certain subjects that I will only speak about briefly, partly to avoid boring you and partly because there are certain areas of debate and conjecture which are beyond the scope of a book like this.

Right, let's start at what I would describe as the beginning for me. In the 1960s, there was a manufacturing boom in Britain, which led to a substantial deficit of unskilled labour. Blighty looked to its former colonies for this workforce, and my dad was precisely the type of cheap, unskilled labourer it desired. He went one step further by also being illiterate. He had arrived from the Mirpur region of rural Pakistan and settled in Bradford, which was the city that required cheap labour more than any other, owing to its vast textile industry. He lived and worked with his fellow Pakistanis and didn't really mix with the indigenous community. The drawback to this was that almost sixty years later, he can only hold basic conversations in English. He was a cross between Kim Jong-un, Roald Dahl, a slightly less enlightened version of the dad from the film *East is East,* and both the Charles Bronsons. The objective of many of his generation was to work hard in Britain for a few years and later return home to use the money. Their existence was grim, as there were many men living in one house, but it was still a lot better than the poverty they had left behind. They lived purely to support their families back in the old country and saved as much as they could to give those people a better life.

The only escape from the rigours of hard graft was at the weekends when they played cards and watched Indian films at cinemas. A legacy from that era is that I've heard my dad refer to the weekly shopping as ration and a 50p coin as ten shillings. In the 1970s, against the advice of the Member of Parliament, Enoch Powell (a man who achieved great notoriety for his views on immigration and integration), my dad made Manningham in Bradford his home by relocating my mum there. He purchased our first house for the same price as his net annual salary, and he was merely a mill worker. Nowadays, an average house of that size will cost about six times the average wage. If anybody from that era complains about how tough they had it, remind them about house prices.

Bradford is now famous for its curries and is named the Curry Capital of Britain almost every year. It is also famous for being the home of the serial killers, the Black Panther, the Crossbow Cannibal (originally from Wakefield, but he lived in Bradford long enough to qualify as a Bradfordian), and the Yorkshire Ripper. Bradford offers great curries, but be careful you don't end up in one. The council should consider this slogan as a welcome sign upon entry into the city. It also has a reputation for being the worst in terms of driving standards in the country, and it's fully deserved. If there is one thing I could change about my hometown, it would be the driving. In the interest of full disclosure, I must admit I haven't driven in every city in the country, but I doubt if there's a place where people drive more dangerously and with total disregard for other road users. There are many who treat the city as one giant race track. Evidence of this is Operation Steerside, which was launched by West Yorkshire Police in Bradford to take positive action against those whose driving fell below the required standards. As far as I am aware, Bradford is the only place to have this type of operation. There are many penalties given out, but it doesn't appear to have made any difference. Anyone who has ever been to Bradford will know precisely what I mean, and it's hardly a fresh observation. It's unsurprising, therefore, why Bradford has some of the highest insurance premiums in the country and why some insurers won't even consider customers from the city.

Bradford is also considered to be the heroin distribution centre of Northern England. The main reasons for this are geography and access. According to various reports, Afghanistan produces approximately 80% of the world's heroin, and, as you may be aware, it shares a large border with Pakistan. You can work out the rest. This drug business is in complete contrast to when I was a child. The only time I heard someone mention drugs was when one of my classmates in upper school mentioned he knew someone who had 'Moroccan Draw.' If a list was compiled (by me anyway), heroin and curry would be first and second as the most addictive things to come out of Pakistan.

Let me recap; if curries, heroin, and driving as though you're being chased by the police are your thing, Bradford is the place for you. If I had to sum up Bradford in one sentence, it would be that if there was a zombie apocalypse in the city centre, nobody would notice. By now, you may have a negative view of my city, but don't despair because it also has a lot going for it. Although I don't have access to official figures, I would say Bradford is the food capital of the North, as it possibly has more food outlets per resident than any other Northern city or town. This isn't limited to curries, and there appears to be a real diversity of food now. It also has some of the most generous people you will find anywhere in the world. You could knock on a random door in inner-city Bradford and expect to be offered food and possibly shelter. This hospitality is probably the reason there are beggars with "homeless" signs standing at practically every set of traffic lights in the inner-city areas. Bradford is my home and my town. I will always defend its good name, but that doesn't mean I won't be honest about its problems.

These problems included rioting in 1995 and 2001 in my area, Manningham. The authorities didn't take any positive action in 1995, and a lot of us were confident of further disorder. They were described at the time as race riots. My honest description would have been that it was idiots destroying their neighbourhoods and fighting with the police because of an assumption they could get away with it. Bradford had looked like a war-zone, with burnt-out shells of vehicles and buildings everywhere. In the aftermath of the 2001 riots, sentences of up to four years were handed out to people who were caught throwing a single stone. Most of the rioters were sheep and merely following others. Young men without any criminal history were criminalised due to a few moments of madness. It sent out a stern message, and twenty years later, there has been nothing remotely comparable to that level of civil unrest, even though many right-wing organisations have had protests here to stir the pot. The riots set the city and race relations back many years. It's debatable whether the economy and reputation of the area ever recovered.

What isn't up for debate is my dad's inability to speak English and also his complete ban on English in our house. It seemed like an attempt to keep out decadent Western values. Televisions were initially also banned for the same reasons. If I wanted to watch television, I had to go to the homes of friends or relatives. Only Punjabi was allowed in our house at that point. By the time I started school, I probably spoke a handful of English words, which were picked up from watching the television. The area I lived in was predominantly Asian, except for a few black and white families. My first school comprised mainly of Asian children, and I don't think any of us spoke English when we started.

My time at school meant I became the first literate person in the history of my family. These new-found skills were a blessing and a burden. My dad decided instead of going to his friends to ask them for help with writing letters and filling forms; he could now use me and my newfound skills for his interpreting and secretarial needs.

The paperwork appeared to be mind-bogglingly complicated, and I felt I was drowning in a well of bureaucracy. My reputation as an interpreter and form-filler spread. Before I knew it, my services were sub-contracted out to our neighbours. If any of my colleagues read this, they could blame my dad for my fear of paperwork. The only opinion heard in my house was my dad's, and I couldn't recall a single meaningful conversation I had with him growing up. It was always him talking and me dreaming of freedom.

In the year 1984, my life was like the one envisioned by George Orwell in his nightmarish dystopian novel named after that year. While Orwell may not have accurately foreseen the degree to which the government would control wider society in the future, his prediction about my life in a totalitarian household was eerily correct. My dad kept an authoritative eye on everything I did. If he ever felt I was becoming British in my attitudes, he would remind me we were Pakistanis and that white people would never accept me as one of their own. He would later cite the war in the Balkans of the early 1990s as absolute proof Muslims would eventually be ethnically cleansed in the West. His logic was that if white Bosnian Muslims, who had been living in the old Yugoslavia for centuries, could be the victims of communal violence, it could certainly happen in Britain. Many people of my dad's generation have espoused the same view over the years.

This belief that Britain could never be home meant that most people built enormous and lavish mansions, costing hundreds of thousands of pounds back home in Pakistan. This was partly due to wanting a home there and partly as a status symbol to show off their perceived wealth. What made this even stranger was that the same people were sometimes living in cramped housing here. The irony of it all is that these people pay someone to live in those mansions and maintain them. This is explained in greater detail in a BBC documentary named 'The Abandoned Mansions of Pakistan,' which is available on YouTube. These types of views meant he wasn't strong on empathy, and we didn't have an open relationship. It was as closed as how Donald Trump imagines all American borders to be in his dreams. Just like Trump, his views would make diversity coordinators squirm and reach for their anti-depressants.

Problems between immigrants and their children are probably a common feature, and it was definitely true in my circle of friends. Only one of my contemporaries had a good relationship with his dad. As in such patriarchal societies, we all respected our fathers due to our culture and faith, but our differences meant we had little in common. An Asian friend described our collective childhoods as those of oppression and subjugation. Those two words sum it up better than anything written by academics on the subject.

Despite all the control, my dad was a wonderful raconteur and would tell us amazing bedtime stories. Everyone would be on the edge of our beds and didn't want the stories to end. We were entertained with exquisitely wrought phrases, deft characterisations, perfect punchlines, and clever plot twists. We would surf on the ebb and flow of his voice. With the right opportunities, he could have had a slightly more glamorous career.

I haven't inherited these vital genes from him, as is abundantly clear to you by now. He has bequeathed me little, apart from baldness (not to be confused with boldness) and British citizenship. This is worth its weight in gold when you consider how much people will pay to be smuggled into the country and how much a British passport is probably worth on the black market. It wasn't worth contemplating what my life would have been like had my dad never made the journey to England.

My wife has already established how this parallel universe would work out for me. According to her, if my dad had remained in Pakistan, I'd be selling tomatoes from a cart and telling everyone my tales of woe. My oiled and bushy handlebar moustache would have a sharp twirl at the tip and wouldn't look out of place if it moonlighted as a squirrel's tail. Because of a lifetime of taking snuff, smoking cigarettes, and chewing betel leaves, my teeth would be every shade of brown imaginable. My style of smoking cigarettes would be to make a fist and then place a cigarette in between my top two fingers. The small gap in the curled-up index finger would then be used up to suck up the smoke, which would be breathed out through my hairy nose. The hairstyle I would adopt would be receding on top, but a straggly mullet at the back, and my shirt would always be unbuttoned at the top to expose a hairy chest. A desire to find a marriage partner in the promised land of England would occupy most of my time. After years of rejection from my first cousins in Britain, I had to settle for my first cousin in Pakistan. She also claimed I would have a lot in common with my wife, such as other cousins, uncles, aunties, grandparents, great-grandparents, and great-great-grandparents. I had to stop her as she could have gone on all night repeating herself.

Incidentally, my parents are actually first cousins, as were my maternal grandparents, and as were probably the generations before that. This would suggest I am the product of centuries of inbreeding. According to my wife, who isn't my cousin or a relative, this practically makes me royalty. She knows how to put things into perspective. If I were to appear on the television show, "Who do you think you are," it would only be 2 minutes long. Going back to moustaches, every boy in my year had a moustache. Moustaches are a common feature in Pakistani culture, and all our fathers had them. Even in those days, I was reluctant to conform and grew a beard to go with the moustache. My wife reckons the real reason for the beard was to obscure my facial features because otherwise, I'd display a circus freak show level of ugliness. Well, it's cheaper than plastic surgery. Her other claim was that I was the only person whose facial features improved when looking at their own reflection in a clean stainless silver spoon. Our marriage wasn't forced, so I don't know what she's complaining about.

Thankfully, my dad made the journey here, and I don't have to think about any parallel universes. His tough upbringing meant he never backed down from a fight. It's highly unlikely he's ever feared another man. If he'd been born a few centuries earlier, he would have been drinking from the skulls of his enemies. Like a lot of men in his circumstances, he was emotionless, unless you consider rage. Even now, his wrists are practically the size of my ankles, and he has the build of a wrestler. I can testify to his heavy-handedness from my personal experience. On the subject of parental chastisement, his policy was to punish first and ask questions later. His capacity for explosive hostility at the slightest perceived offence was legendary. One poignant example of this is from my early teens when my dad saw a man swearing at his friend on our street. My dad threatened to slap this man, which caused the man to turn around in fear and walk back into his house. My dad worked the night shift in a mill, and later that night, someone hurled a brick through our window. It was almost certainly the same man, who probably felt this was his only method of retribution. This might not seem particularly courageous, but this guy had serious mental health issues. A lot of his time had been shared between hospitals and prison. His latest prison sentence had been for stabbing someone in a pub. Even someone like him, who wasn't completely in control of his senses, knew he would struggle in a physical altercation with my dad. That man (not my dad) was a ticking time bomb, which sadly went off in 2003 when he bludgeoned his elderly mother to death.

Our street was peaceful, apart from one family who tested everyone's toughness and particularly my dad's. The father was a trouble-causer, and his four sons were totally out of control. During one of their many incidents of terrible behaviour, they were throwing stones at an elderly lady. One stone struck my baby brother on the head, which needed medical attention. When my dad returned home and found out, he didn't say a word but was trembling with rage, and I knew he would take robust action. He went upstairs for a minute and then walked out of the front door. My dad returned home minutes later, dripping with blood from his hands. He asked me to ring the police to report that the father of the boys who had injured my brother had stabbed him. For a man who had been stabbed, he was remarkably composed. His alleged assailant had made a counter allegation, and they took both parties to the police station. The police investigation fully exonerated my dad from any wrong-doing as there weren't any witnesses who came forward, even though half the street claimed to have been present. My dad never had any police involvement previously, unlike his adversary, who was well known to the police. This incident left the other guy with one long stab wound to his chest. His portly build had saved him from certain death but resulted in him receiving lengthy hospital treatment. My dad's version of events was that he had gone merely to speak to him about the behaviour of his children but had been met with hostility. The other chap had then brandished a flick knife, which led to a violent struggle. The flick knife was never found. Almost the entire street came to thank my dad. One person even offered his services and weapons to assist if any further violence was needed against the same man. There wasn't any further trouble, and the family moved out a short time later. I wish I had the strength and valour of my dad.

One aspect of life where I didn't want to be like my dad was his diet. The only thing he's really eaten as a main meal during his life is curry. Ask any person of Pakistani origin what their meals consisted of in the 1970s, 80s, and 90s, and they would tell you it was almost certainly curry twice a day, every day. Breakfast was the only time we didn't have curry. I had curry about fourteen times a week during the school holidays. This routine was sometimes broken by homemade chips. We considered chips a treat and seemed like the height of fine dining. Curry is probably Britain's national dish now, but I remember hating it and wanting English food instead. The curries on weekdays were normally lentils and vegetables but chicken or mutton on weekends, in case there were any visitors. It was considered cheap to offer guests vegetarian curries.

If you asked me what I had for my evening meal on the first Saturday of January 1982, I could guarantee it was some type of curry. We didn't have forks because Pakistani food didn't require them. It was customary in that part of the world to eat with hands unless it required a spoon. It was left to the school dinner ladies to teach me English dining etiquette. For many years, I rejoiced in the belief I had complete mastery of knives and forks. This was until a colleague enquired why I held my knife and fork in the wrong hands. Were there government guidelines on what to hold in which hand? I wasn't aware of any. Foods such as mash potato, fish fingers, beans, and pudding with custard seemed like the holy grail of exotic cuisine. The school dinner was undoubtedly the highlight of the day. Like a lot of schools, they expected us to finish our plates, not that it was ever an issue for a greedy person like myself. The only time food was plentiful was at Asian weddings. Even though it was a time of relative poverty, weddings were still extravagant. This was to project an illusion of affluence, and people spent well beyond their means. They were many children who gate-crashed weddings because it was so easy to get lost in a sea of guests.

The economic hardship of Asian families was exacerbated by the decline of the manufacturing industry in the 1970s and 80s. It hit the generally unskilled, non-English speaking Pakistani workers harder than the indigenous communities. Some diversified into taxi driving and curry houses, but many suffered the indignity of unemployment for the remainder of their days. Those who worked in curry houses were paid only a fraction of what was paid in other food industries. This work generally wasn't declared to the authorities, and the criminally low-paid curry house worker had no choice but to claim unemployment benefits. As Asian families were quite big, it made their economic situation even worse. The vast majority of my Asian schoolmates were on free dinners at school because of their parents' unemployment. There was also a noticeable difference between the living standards of those families who had people to support in Pakistan and those who didn't. My dad didn't have any brothers here to share the economic burden of Pakistan and therefore had to subsidise his relatives on his own. Thankfully, he was one of the fortunate ones, as his mill carried on trading into the 21st century. These economic hardships meant most Pakistani families had a tab with their local shopkeeper, who was paid at the end of every week. For openness and transparency, the customer and the shopkeeper would have their own books, and entries would be made in both.

The shopkeeper provided not merely essential household items for struggling families but also filled out forms for them. It was a frugal and threadbare existence, only by Western European standards though. My shopkeeper wrote letters on my dad's behalf when I had to explain why I had missed school or was late. The teachers would have easily recognised my atrocious handwriting. Those who wear a certain type of tinted glasses might describe that period as the golden age for British Pakistanis. While I didn't agree with this sentiment, there were aspects of that period I missed deeply. Sorry for the cliché, but there was a genuine sense of community spirit. People visited each other's houses regularly and didn't feel they were intruding if they ate at neighbour's or friend's houses. Food was routinely shared with neighbouring houses. We considered even third or fourth cousins to be like brothers or sisters unless we married them. Everyone knew each other, whereas now, I've only spoken to my neighbour once.

In the late 1970s and early 1980s, as well as the food,

the only entertainment offered to me, had a distinct Asian flavour to it. Indian films became my favourite form of entertainment, particularly at the cinema. Apart from my favourite film, 'Sholay,' all the other films had poor production quality, but I loved the unmatched escapism they provided. It was pure fantasy and unbelievably far-fetched. They were normally about brothers who had been separated at birth and were somehow reunited at the end to kill the villain(s). Pakistani films were of even poorer quality, and I don't think I've ever watched a full one. My dad didn't want to take me to the cinema because I was a bed-wetter, and he believed this meant I was a cinema-wetter too. It was left to my cousin to take me.

My cousin was a real hard case and obsessed with fighting and training. It was obvious to him I was a weakling, and he made me do exercises most days to toughen me up. I had a personal trainer before it became fashionable. When I was made to do press-ups at school, the teacher singled me out because I had the best technique. Despite this, I was still a physical weakling. My cousin was like an older brother I never had and was everything I wanted to be. Everyone seemed to know him, and he had a lot of friends. He moved down South in his late teens, which instantly made him busy. If he hadn't moved, I'd have been a far more confident person and would have had some confidence in a physical altercation.

The Indian films were always over three hours long

and therefore needed breaks midway when viewed at the cinema. The cinemas would offer fresh samosas, Bombay mix, and Coca-Cola in glass bottles as snacks during the breaks. Coca-Cola was not as dark as it is now; it was much fizzier and tasted a lot better. This was in the days before cinema food became criminally expensive.

It was also a common custom for Asian families to hire a video player, along with about six Indian or Pakistani films, on the weekends. Those weekends were dedicated entirely to these films, and I remember staying up all night with the adults to get through every single one. Only the well-off could afford to buy their own video players or colour televisions. My summers were spent in Newcastle at my mum's cousin's house. He owned the two afore-mentioned luxury items. He was an old-school wheeler and dealer who invested in property at an early age. It felt like an all-inclusive holiday because food was aplenty there too. It was easily the happiest part of my childhood. My dad briefly toyed with the idea of moving there, and if he had, you'd have been reading Once Upon a Time in Bradford and Newcastle. I was very close to my second cousins from Newcastle at the time, but after a family dispute in the mid-1980s, I never went back. We've only seen each other a handful of times over the years and have little in common now.

What I wanted more than anything in the world at the time was our own television. After much nagging, my dad finally relented and brought home a small black and white television, which was placed on a shelf high on the wall and was practically touching the ceiling. That was the best place for the little aerial to get the strongest signal. It meant I had to stand up and watch it from a lot closer, which affected my eyesight. The other issue was that I had to stand on something or use a stick to switch the channels. There were only three channels, and I didn't have to change the channel often. BBC1 and ITV were the only channels we watched because BBC2 was arty and had nothing for the likes of myself. It wasn't the sort of television that would come with a remote control, but it should have come with some binoculars instead.

The introduction of the television in our house meant my dad took too much interest in the news and elected me his political analyst. This was strange because none of it affected him unless the news item was about the decline of the textile industry in Britain. Needless to say, I carried out my task with obedience but without enthusiasm. He couldn't quite fathom how I could sum up in ten seconds what it took the newsreader to say in five minutes. He would give me a bemused look, which suggested he thought I was either an amazing interpreter or a compulsive liar. If I appeared to struggle with my interpreting duties, he would ask if I was learning any English at school. I wanted my dad's ban on English in our house to be enforced more stringently when the news was on and not only when it suited him.

After he had left for work, I would sneak downstairs to watch the television until they stopped broadcasting, which was around midnight. This contributed to me feeling tired at school. About 15 years later, I found an old school report where the teacher questioned whether I was getting enough sleep. Watching television became even more fun than playing out, and I spent the vast majority of my waking life doing exactly that. The one time we would watch television together as a family was at 4 pm on Saturdays when the wrestling was on. The main wrestlers were Big Daddy and Giant Haystacks. They were fat, hairy men and built totally different from their American counterparts. At the time, I believed it was real and also thought it was cool to be obese.

My favourite show was 'The Incredible Hulk,' because it was about a small, weedy man who could transform himself into an unbelievably powerful monster when he was in danger. I was so small and weedy that even some girls at school were taller than me. Until the age of 15, I was only 5'1" tall but thankfully shot up nine inches in one year to reach my current height. The Incredible Hulk was later overtaken by my all-time favourite television show, 'Blackadder' (only series 2 and 4), which was about an amazingly witty man who was as funny as a clever simile.

My television viewing was seriously hindered when I was made to go to the local mosque for Islamic studies straight after school. This was every single weekday for an hour and a half and two-and-a-half hours on Saturday mornings. It was an archaic studying system, and young children were routinely caned on their hands for mispronouncing some words from the Qur'an. All the teachers were imported from the Indian subcontinent, and they didn't speak any English. One of those teachers was particularly sadistic, and he nipped people instead of caning them. This led to his acquisition of the nickname 'Jack the Nipper.' As I'll explain later, physical punishment also happened in schools, but nowhere near on the same scale. Both went unquestioned. All I knew was that I was being forced to read some holy book, and that was it. This system of learning caused me to question my faith, and I almost rejected it. It wasn't until I left the mosque that I discovered for myself what my faith was truly about.

Mosques are run a lot more professionally nowadays, and physical abuse is unheard of. They even allow kids to play sports and give holidays in line with state schools. The 1970s and 1980s were, however, harsher and less sensitive times.

A lot of children of my generation spent practically every spare moment playing outside and would only return home for food and liquid replenishments. When the girls reached their teens, they were generally not allowed to go out at all, apart from school. Some were sent to Pakistan, and practically all were made to leave school at 16 years old. The natural progression was for them to be then taken to Pakistan to get married (normally to a first cousin). Most of these marriages were decided at birth. Pakistani culture dictates children should obey their parents when it comes to marriage, but Islam clearly states it should be a personal choice. Whether the marriages were forced or not is something I'll leave for you to decide. The whole point of taking the girls to Pakistan in those days was to protect them from boys and also stop any Western influences. An unmarried adult daughter was considered at risk of bringing dishonour to the family in case she started to develop ideas of freedom and if she somehow came into contact with boys. If there wasn't a first cousin available, there would be a queue of suitors desperate for a better life in England. For these reasons, marriages were rushed. Boys were also taken to Pakistan to keep ties with their relatives and their "homeland." They were also taken again later for marriage. I can recall only one boy from my age group who married a girl from the UK, but all the rest went to Pakistan for arranged/ forced marriages. The misery of those being forced was compounded when Tony Blair's Labour party came into power in 1997. Blair's party had made promises to the Asian electorate that they would remove something called the Primary Purpose Rule if they got into power, which would make it much easier to obtain spouse visas. Prior to 1997, anyone applying for a spouse visa had to prove that the primary purpose of the marriage was not to gain entry into the UK. When the rule was in place, spouse visas had taken years to be issued, but after that year, they were issued in weeks. Before the 2001 election, I was woken from my sleep by Labour Party activists who were canvassing in Urdu through a loudspeaker in a vehicle. The speaker claimed that if the Conservative Party got into power, they would be bringing back the Primary Purpose Rule. The canvasser knew which political issues really mattered to the Pakistani voters.

There were girls who rebelled and fought for their right to marry someone of their choice. They risked death by running away and bringing dishonour to their families. These families did everything they could to protect this honour and literally believed in death before dishonour. This created business opportunities for self-styled 'Bounty Hunters' to bring the girls back by force. One such individual was named Tahir, and had a television documentary made about him. Even though he was from Huddersfield, he conducted a lot of his business in Bradford. If your mind was conjuring up images of Dog, the Bounty Hunter, or Clint Eastwood from a western, you needed to think again. This man was a chain-smoking, heavy-breathing, overweight, balding man with long hair at the sides. He had claimed to have informants working in the Benefits Agency who would furnish him with addresses of runaway girls. He also claimed he never hit the girls but admitted to threatening them. Among his team was a Karate practitioner, and I suspect he wasn't there for his investigative skills. This video can be found on YouTube under the title, 'The Bounty Hunter Documentary by Asad Qureshi.'

At the age of nine, I moved to middle school, and the choice of school was based on only one criterion, geography. Just like my parents, all my friends' parents wanted to send them to the schools that were the closest to their houses. Drummond Middle School was chosen for me. My teacher in the first year was Miss Vickers, who was wonderful and extremely generous. She would take us to the nearby Lister Park, where she would read books to us as we sat on the grass. The most memorable book was *The Fib* and *Other Stories* by George Layton. It was the best book I'd ever read or heard because it captured the viewpoint of the child better than anything I'd known. He instantly became my favourite writer. Many years later, I discovered he was from Bradford, and quite recently, I discovered he was also from Manningham and brought up a few streets way from me. He was also of immigrant stock. In 1960, when he was in his late teens, he left Bradford for drama school in London. His parents didn't move from his childhood home until the mid-1980s, which happened to be on the same street as my local mosque. It's possible our paths may have crossed when he visited his parents. It wasn't only as an author that he is known, because he starred in many television shows, such as Minder and It Ain't Half Hot Mum. His talents weren't limited to writing books and acting. He also created two BBC situation comedies, *Don't Wait Up* and *Executive*

Stress. It is pointless to list all his achievements here, as you can Google it yourself if you care to. To top it off, we both attended Lilycroft First School. That is all strangely coincidental and about as believable as an empty browser history.

Whilst in the park, Miss Vickers would buy everyone a lolly from the ice-cream van. My first thought was that she must be rich. But it turned out she wasn't rich, because I asked her. She wasn't poor either because I asked her that too. It turned out she was something called 'comfortable.'

My biggest debt of gratitude to Miss Vickers wasn't just the lollies but that she helped me solve a problem afflicting most native speakers of Asian languages. In those languages, there isn't any differentiation between the v and w sounds. It is entirely interchangeable. She explained, in painstaking detail, that in English, we should pronounce the v by touching the top teeth with the bottom lip and pronounce the w with the lips only. She was the first teacher to help me with this, even though I was nine years old at the time. In the second year, my form teacher was Mr Bentley, and his teaching style was the total opposite of Miss Vickers. He didn't believe in second chances and would slap the bottoms of boys after any type of indiscretion.

The headteacher at the school was named Ray Honeyford, and the deputy head was Fred Edmondson. These two men would both become famous for different reasons. Mr Edmondson, or 'Egghead' as he was nicknamed because of the shape of his bald head, was a strict disciplinarian. He used a shoe, which he affectionately named Rupert, to dish out punishment. Their relationship was more pet and owner than footwear and wearer. His glasses were always hanging off the tip of his nose, and it was a miracle because they never slipped off. He was the father of a Bradford-born actor, Adrian Edmondson, who would later talk about his problematic relationship with his disciplinarian father, but they made up years later. Honeyford became famous because he had written articles for a magazine named The Salisbury Review about some failings of multiculturalism. Among his concerns was that children of Pakistani heritage couldn't speak English by the time they started school. He also had issues with children being taken to Pakistan for long periods, and therefore, they missed important schooling. In a school where approximately 99% of the pupils were of Pakistani origin, it wouldn't end well for him. This led to protests and demands for his resignation. Community leaders, who were generally appointed due to their caste rather than merit, bullied parents or coerced them, at the very least, into a complete boycott of the school.

On the subject of the caste system, it absolutely exists in the older generation, especially to those who consider themselves to be of a higher caste. It doesn't exist in the way it does in certain parts of India, where the lowest castes aren't allowed to mix with mainstream society. Its existence is in a much milder form in Pakistani society, where there is sometimes a belief that those born into a lower caste are not of as good character as those born into higher castes. Pakistan used to be a part of India until 1947, and the culture of the two countries is very similar. This is why the caste system still exists in Pakistani society. It is a system that goes against Islamic beliefs, which state that a person should only be judged by their character. The younger generation doesn't care for the caste system, and it is slowly being eroded in Britain.

Back at Drummond Middle School, there were banners comparing Honeyford's actions with that of the Apartheid regime of the South African government. It was big enough news for the BBC show, Panorama, to make a programme about it. We were then taken to study at the nearby Pakistani Community Centre. The classes were disorganised, and it seemed like time off.

At the Pakistani Community Centre, we were given, as you would guess, curry. I was desperate to go back to Drummond and the school dinners, but I didn't fancy being a political martyr. The whole affair seemed to last forever, and my culinary needs were being severely neglected. Margaret Thatcher, the then Prime Minister, even got involved in the saga. Honeyford was dismissed, reinstated then ultimately forced to take early retirement with a golden handshake. According to one teacher (not Honeyford), the school had to change its policy of standing assemblies because some children were fainting. This was due to Asian children not having any breakfast. There was definitely some truth to this. The new headmaster came in and spoke about the benefits of being bilingual. Clearly a handpicked, company man. Nobody could blame him if he wanted a quiet life. In the early 1990s, Channel 4 made a television film named 'Northern Crescent,' which was based loosely on the Honeyford story.

It was a depressing time, and my obsessive character needed an obsession to relieve the boredom. Indian films had lost their appeal by then due to what felt to me like unrealistic stories, and football became my new form of escapism. I've never met anybody who had a greater devotion or passion for the game as I did. It was the ultimate test of machismo, style, and artistry. It's shameful to admit it now, but it became more important to me than even my family. My hometown club, Bradford City, was the logical choice of team to support. Unlike most football obsessives, there was something holding me back. I was undeniably the worst player I had ever known.

As I got older, I was struck with the grim reality that I was as useless at everything else as I was at football. My role in the film of life would be that of an unnamed extra. One advantage of this knowledge was that I didn't place any pressure on myself to achieve anything. Sadly, the same thing couldn't be said of my dad because he had epically delusional expectations of me. This was based on his assumption that if I had any type of schooling, it automatically made me a boffin.

It's possible he'd seen my handwriting and instantly concluded, "Doctor." His lectures were virtually a daily occurrence and didn't adopt the cajoling approach. It was a constant game of cat and mouse to avoid him and his lectures. He also adopted the same tactic to espouse the virtues of marrying first cousins and keeping it in the family. To strengthen his case, he would give me examples of broken marriages, which were a direct result of people not marrying first cousins. His belief was that you knew what you were getting with first cousins, whereas outsiders would ultimately show their disloyalty. He also viewed not marrying first cousins (providing one was available) as an act of betrayal against the auntie or uncle who might become the mother or father-in-law. Not to mention that the person refusing marriage would be preventing their cousin from having a better life in Britain. The irony of ironies was that my dad didn't actually have any nieces or nephews, but my mum did.

This practice is native to that part of the world, and the Islamic perspective on this is the same as British law, as it's neither endorsed nor prohibited. Another common practice was for young widows to marry the brother of their dead husband to keep any wealth within the family. There will be occasions of honesty in the book, normally reserved for those at the end of a five-day alcoholic binge or someone about to be given their last rites. Hopefully, my openness won't start mass protests, book and effigy burnings or lead to fatwas being issued against me, either from royalists or other purveyors of cousin-marrying.

My inability to swim, skip, climb, play any sport or ride a bike added to my lack of confidence. I didn't possess any flexibility or physical coordination to speak of. My knowledge of computers is rudimentary, and I consider any three-year-old child as tech support. Asking me to work on an electronic device is equal to an average person trying to hack Edward Snowden's emails. No matter what I did, I constantly had a sense of nervous inadequacy. I consider myself a grand theoretician on the subject of being rubbish at everything. My usefulness in life was on a par with a ponytail on a bald man. The only thing I wasn't absolutely rubbish at was English, and my spelling can be best described as ever so slightly above average.

My build was something supermodels could only fantasise about, and I didn't even have to make myself vomit. I had the physical strength of a cheap balloon. It took me longer to pass my driving test than anyone I knew. Let's not even bother talking about my lack of home maintenance skills. If anything needed fixing in my house, my wife did it unless it wasn't electrical. I will elaborate on the electric business later. She described me as the quintessential slob because my personal habits would make a monkey blush.

Her domineering personality is something brutal dictators could learn from. I would describe her as more of a carer than a wife, and my resourcefulness (or lack thereof) is such that I would struggle to survive a day without her in the real world. If left to my own devices, I would suffer from self-neglect in a bed-sit. My life would consist of baked beans, endless repeats of Jeremy Kyle, and my odour would be enough to make the fleas on a sewer rat poorly. There would be empty cans, pizza boxes, and pistachio shells strewn everywhere. When I was young, my mum did everything for me. When I got married, my wife took over. As a result of this, I have never used an iron, washing machine, dishwasher, or vacuum cleaner. This doesn't make me a misogynist but a product of my environment.

Despite all my problems, I have an almost photographic memory for facts and details, but this only applies to useless information. It still isn't anywhere near as good as my wife's memory, where my faults and mistakes are concerned. She treats every conversation with me like a police interview from the 1970s, without a solicitor, a lot of falsified evidence, and a complete dismissal of key witnesses. My house might as well have egg shells instead of carpets. If I'm murdered, I want her to be the senior investigator unless evidence points to her being the prime suspect. As you will soon realise, other good suspects would emerge. She has the skills to solve any murder, specifically if it was made personal, because the murderer had questioned her choice of home décor or had made negative comments about her culinary skills.

As well as my wife, there have been others who have

caused me to feel fear. When I started Belle Vue Boys' Upper School, one boy made it his business to bully me mercilessly. It was never anything physical, but I was constantly threatened with violence, which seemed worse than actual violence. The threats were sufficient to bend or snap my puny will. He'd tell me even his farts were stronger than me, which was unnecessary and trying to prove it was certainly unnecessary. He absolutely outdid himself when he duped someone from my street into knocking on my door by convincing the duped party that he was my friend. The bully didn't live close to me, and he would have had to make numerous enquiries to locate my address. This showed a degree of commitment to bullying, which I found worrying but also slightly admirable. This sudden escalation was to demonstrate to me I was never safe from him. "Why are you doing this?" I asked inquisitively to gain some measure of his psyche. His response was clinical, ruthless, and slightly disturbing, "Because I am a very bad person, and I can."

That night I slumped on my bed like a humiliated heap and didn't sleep a wink, struggling to identify a way to end the ordeal. There was no reasoning with him; violence was the only answer. For someone who was wetter than an alcoholic's toilet seat, fighting would not come naturally. If there was ever a fight, I would be the last person to be summoned to help, right after the elderly canteen lady at the Samaritans office. Why couldn't I be more like my dad or my cousin? Actually,

I'd have gladly been anyone but myself; if only I wasn't the patron saint of cowardice. I even composed a list of people in my head who could help me. This included a psychiatrist, assertiveness coach, martial arts trainer, and my personal favourite, hiring a bigger bully to beat up my bully. The last option would require money, but my meagre resources meant I ruled it out. What's the worst that could happen? He might beat me up, but at least he would realise I was willing to fight back. That would surely cause him to find someone more vulnerable to pick on. The only issue was that I couldn't think of anyone more vulnerable at the school who would be more afraid to fight back. I was a low-hanging fruit, as far as he was concerned. Either it was going to end that day, or it was going to escalate. Standing up for myself was something I hadn't done since, wait a minute, there was the stark realisation I'd never stood up for myself or been in a physical altercation.

He was bigger and presumably stronger than I was, but I could use the element of surprise. The next day, we had our English class in the library, and he was sitting next to me. He had previously written about how, on a bright cloudy day, he had gone with his family to Luxembourg and played on the sandy white beaches. He would break off for a few seconds and whisper his customary threats while I wearily sat next to him. While he was looking down at his book and probably about to write about how he was going to conquer the Polar ice caps of Texas, I punched him in the face as hard and in as quick succession as I could. I was incandescent with rage, and it was time to let out all the fury. It was like I was in a trance, and it wasn't me punching him. He shielded his face, and the teacher pulled me off. There were tears running down his face, and he seemed visibly distraught. A few minutes later, when the adrenaline wore off, my hand looked like it had been injected with helium. Further evidence of why I wasn't cut out for violence. He didn't appear to have a mark on his face. We didn't become friends after the incident, but we both carried on as though the bullying or the library incident had never taken place. My levels of bravery had progressed from non-existent to minuscule. I saw him a couple of years ago, and I was in Poundland with my son. He had taken up triathlons, where he ran, swam, and cycled great distances. Due to this training, he didn't appear to have much body fat and was extremely lean. I explained to my son that this was the bully I had told him about. His response was, "How could you let a skinny guy like him bully you?"

The other bully I encountered was also from my time at the same school. His modus operandi was to sneak in behind me and slap me quite hard to the top of my head. I can blame him for my baldness as much as my dad's genes. There wasn't a heroic ending to this story, as the bully was too big to confront. If I had tried to attack him, even with weapons, the most I would have achieved would have been to put his tie slightly out of place. The risk and reward didn't add up. He once threatened a posh supply teacher with, "I'll slap yer daft." The confused teacher asked, "Pardon, you are going to slap my daft?"

Violence seemed like an anti-boredom device to him, and he was totally unhinged. During one altercation, he picked up the nearest thing to him to throw at the other guy. The nearest thing on this occasion was a small boy from a few years below. With the technique of an inept shot putter, the bully picked up the little boy and launched him at his competitor. Nobody was injured during this incident, but it showed he had little regard for the sanctity of human life. The bullying only lasted a few months, but it left a mark on me right at the top of my head. He claimed to be the proud possessor of a GCSE grade A in slapping heads.

When the time for our actual GSCE exams approached, we were advised by the teachers to check our passports and birth certificates for our 'official' names because those names didn't always match those we used at school. The teachers were concerned we would have the wrong names on our academic certificates if we got any. Upon checking, all of my six closest friends discovered we had all been using the wrong names. For some, it was a simple spelling mistake, and others had a prefix of Mohammed they didn't know about, while a few had different surnames to their fathers. This was mainly because our illiterate fathers struggled to spell, and surnames aren't shared by family members in Pakistani culture as they are in

Western culture. Some went as far as to change their names by deed poll for ease and convenience.

As the 1980s were ending, hope was on the horizon. This might sound a little melodramatic, but the economic situation of many people in my area changed around 1990 when a cut-price Scandinavian supermarket named 'Netto' arrived. It was especially welcome because, in 1990, bank interest rates were at an all-time high. 'Netto' prices were usually half and occasionally a third of other supermarkets. Bread was sold for as little as 9p, and everything else was equally cheap. My local shopkeeper even shopped there and then sold the items in his shop. There appeared to be more of everything, and it could have also been the start of obesity. Our area had quickly gone up from what I'd describe as lower working class to middle working class. 'Netto' should have been given a humanitarian award for what they did in inner-city Bradford.

THE CHAPTER ABOUT MY OBSESSION WITH MY CHILDHOOD HERO

You may now wonder why I was obsessed with some random football player named Des Walker. As soon as I saw him play, I realised that a lack of ball skills wasn't a barrier to playing football, and being able to defend was just as important. He never wanted the ball and would try to give it to the nearest teammate at every opportunity. In all my days of watching football, I'd never seen anyone with this style of play. He was a defender, and all he cared about was defending his goal.

It wasn't evident if he had really poor ball control, but it appeared as though he didn't want it to be tested. Whenever he had the ball, he passed it to the nearest teammate. He was regarded to be one of the fastest men in football, and early in his career, the Nottingham Forest fans coined the now famous "You'll never beat Des Walker" chant. This was how much confidence the fans had in him. He would also routinely out-jump much taller strikers due to his prodigious leap, and this made him equally difficult to beat in the air as on the ground. He could read the game like a psychic, and his tackles were cleaner than a vegetarian's red chopping board. It was as though he'd been created by scientists in a laboratory for the express purpose of preventing goals. He was like a superhero to me, and I was expecting a Des Walker costume to be released. To me, Des Walker became bigger than football, and I modelled myself on him until, in my mind, I became Des Walker.

My position in the picking order for street football surged upwards, and I made the starting line-up. Playing football became enjoyable, and I grew in confidence. This didn't mean I had become a confident person. It would require more than Des Walker to accomplish that. He definitely made me feel better about myself, though. Bizarrely, I became quite a fast runner at roughly the same time. It was gratifying to spoil things for the talented players. Just like Des, I hated being taken on or beaten and would take it personally.

This story has the makings of a documentary, a feel-good-movie, a Netflix original mini-series, and even a Broadway musical. In the modern age of diversity and inclusivity, it would probably be interpreted as a romantic comedy starring Morgan Freeman and Jane Seymour.

Little is, however, known about Des, as he has been intensely private his whole career and has seldom granted interviews. This made my quest for information virtually impossible in the pre-internet era. It's still difficult now. Sadly, I had picked the least accessible, modern-era English player.

I was practically camped at my local library to check football magazines and newspapers, hoping to find out more about him. A lot of my formative years were spent in that library, along with quite a few homeless people who were generally trying to avoid the harsh winter conditions. When there was an absence of a television in our house, I found solace and escapism in books from there. As an act of gratitude, I plan to donate a copy of my book to the same library. If any fellow sad and laughable individuals happen to come across this book while trying to keep warm in Manningham Library, I hope you feel better about yourself…because you're not me. Or you could just be grateful you won't have to sit on a wobbly chair or sofa while you're there.

Des helped England qualify for the 1990 World Cup in Italy and became an indispensable member of the team. The BBC got the country into the mood by choosing Nessun Dorma as their World Cup theme tune. It went on to become synonymous with football worldwide. England made it all the way to the semi-finals, and Des was considered one of the best players in the tournament. This was a time when I didn't know another Asian person who supported England in any sport. This is in complete contrast to nowadays, where every young Asian football fan I know supports England.

The most significant moment of the World Cup for me was England's first game against the Republic of Ireland. It's generally regarded as the worst game in the history of the World Cup. My description of what I observed on the pitch that day became eerily correct after it was revealed many years later by Gary Lineker himself that he was suffering from diarrhoea and had sprayed the pitch with his own brand of fertiliser. He could be observed wiping his backside and his hands on the pitch. I must have received some type of subliminal message, and the word I had used to describe the game wasn't diarrhoea but something with similar composition. Luckily for Lineker, England were wearing dark shorts, and he masked his embarrassment as well as his discharges quite well. He should have received a yellow card for fouling, at least. In his defence, he scored the only England goal, even though it was sloppy, so I suppose the juice was worth the squeeze. Pardon the pungency. The well of Gary Lineker's diarrhoea jokes will be bled dry by the time I'm finished, but it's my book, and I can do as I please.

Fast forward to 1993, Des played for England against Holland in an important qualifier for the 1994 World Cup. It's a game I'll remember until my dying day unless Alzheimer's gets me first. England was winning the game by two goals to one, and Des got into a race with a player named Marc Overmars. Des had a decent lead, but I watched with stunned horror as Overmars became a blur and easily went past Des. By comparison, Des seemed slower than the speed of dark or a 1993 internet connection. Des pulled Overmars' shirt and gave away a penalty, which was converted, and the match ended in a draw. Football would never be the same for me.

England played against Poland a month later in another important game, and Des got into another foot race in a similar position. This time with Dariusz Adamczuk, who easily ran past him to score. England got a late equaliser to salvage a draw. The belief amongst the footballing community was that Des had lost his famous pace, but the reality was that he had the misfortune to come up against two of the fastest players in the world. He had been outpaced twice in two games, and both incidents had led to important goals. A few days later, England played against Norway, and Des went to tackle a player but gave away a free kick. Des stayed to remonstrate with the official, but the Norwegians took a quick free kick and scored. England lost the game, and England failed to qualify for the 1994 World Cup. His troubles consumed a lot of my time and a lot more than they had any right to. It is unclear how depressed Des was in 1993, but I can confirm I was extremely depressed. It still haunts me to this day. If I had chosen another player to model myself on, I wouldn't have suffered the great depression of 1993. It kept me up most nights, and it was frequently the first thing I thought about when I woke up. It was obviously a lot worse for Des, but I wish I hadn't been dragged into the whole affair.

THE CHAPTER ABOUT HOW I BECAME A COMPLETE AND UTTER DANKA

Although Des and I were both struggling in a footballing sense around this time, I secured my first full-time employment. It was obvious from an early age I would probably spend my time in low-paid, menial work, and that was what happened. It was that or jump on the nearest scrap heap because there was a long-term recession ongoing. Morrisons and Netto had already turned me down for the lofty positions of shelf stacker and general dogsbody. Anything more than a menial job seemed like a ridiculously long shot, and I didn't want the embarrassment of looking to the state to provide me with sustenance. My job entailed opening the post at a prominent bank in Bradford. The post room had been outsourced to an external company named 'Danka.' I was, therefore, about to become a complete and utter Danka. A role many would have said I was perfectly suited to. The 6am starts meant there weren't many takers, and thankfully for me, they took almost anyone on, but I still didn't fancy my chances. The interview started well because the person before me didn't even bother turning up and mine started early. Although, I was concerned my chances had taken a hit when I was quizzed about my career aspirations if I was successful. My response of "not getting sacked" wasn't received in the jovial manner it was intended. It made one interviewer make notes, although I suspect he was ticking boxes. I've always considered myself the box-ticking alternative. The interview must have gone well because I was offered the job the same day.

As I entered the post room on my first day, I saw a big sign above the entrance, which read, "IF YOU'RE NOT PREPARED TO BITE A COLLEAGUE'S HEAD OFF AND SH*T DOWN THEIR THROAT FOR YOUR OWN SELFISH GAIN, WE SUGGEST YOU TURN AROUND AND NEVER COME BACK." It wouldn't have surprised me if it was in the small print of the contract I'd signed. For a few seconds, I viewed the sign and asked myself if I was prepared to descend to such depths of depravity. Absolutely, I thought, I'm up for such japes and frolics. The sign might have had some religious significance because some people touched the sign before every shift.

My job was to open the mortgage-related post and divide it into correspondence with cheques and correspondence without cheques. Some of us still got this wrong. They would then split the post without cheques into five different departments. One particular customer was very creative and used to attach a detailed letter to his cheque, which would include a late repayment fee. It always started off with, "YOU COMPLETE AND UTTER ******S." He had a different expletive in the opening line every time he wrote a letter. The letters were basically a tirade against Western imperialism, the banking system, and a whole host of conspiracy theories. He wished agonising deaths upon all bank employees. As Dankas, we weren't actually employed by the bank, so we agreed with him. The funnier letters were read out to the whole post room.

The place was a gossip monger's dream. Any juicy information gleaned from private and confidential envelopes that had been mistakenly opened was circulated throughout the whole building faster than the speed of light. Some rumours and gossip gained such traction that they were unrecognisable from what was first read on paper. It was said that in the post room, even the blades on the letter opening machine had ears.

The place had a level of complacency, negligence, and insubordination that had probably rarely been shown during human history. There was enough skulduggery and Machiavellianism entrenched in the culture of the post room to make a Shakespearean villain run to the nearest confessional. Nobody had anyone's back unless it was for the express purpose of stabbing it. It wasn't a dog-eat-dog world because dogs don't actually eat other dogs. After hours of research on highly credible websites, I concluded that chimpanzees are possibly the worst offenders at eating their own kind, and therefore, it was a chimpanzee-eat-chimpanzee world. Snide comments were a part of virtually every conversation, and there was a perpetual cycle of one-upmanship. It was a place where, if you kicked any random person violently to the backside, you would rejoice safely in the knowledge they deserved it, and they would be relieved of any constipation. The curious paradox was that almost everyone appeared to be happy to work there. The post room was at the bottom of the organisation, literally and figuratively, because we occupied the ground floor. When I explained to my mate, Kamran, how cushy it all was, he joined me.

The general post was sorted by people, everyone referred to as "The Big Dankas." They were mostly men in their fifties who had been working there since the bank was a small building society and their views were as old as the building itself. They openly admitted to massaging the post figures with a skill of a Turkish masseur to keep themselves in jobs. They had mastered the art of looking busy while doing nothing. A lot of their time was spent drinking tea and wandering around with envelopes in their hands. If they were 'Big Dankas,' naturally, we were 'Baby Dankas.'

As I gained experience, I made it my business to seek every loophole in the process possible, like a bounty hunter. My corner cutting reached such extremes I might as well have carried my personal guillotine because a pair of scissors wouldn't have cut it. I could do the work in my sleep, and I did it frequently because I regularly fell asleep at the sorting table. Sometimes I considered buying some dark sunglasses to wear at work to avoid getting caught as I slept. The 6 am starts weren't ideal for a nocturnal being such as myself, but it all seemed worthwhile with the early finish. Kamran never slept at work. He couldn't afford to because his snoring would have been heard on the seventh floor. When his family went on a holiday, he asked me to stay the night at his house to keep him and his brother company. The next morning, I was woken by what I thought were workmen drilling outside. I was livid that the council would allow their workmen to start at 6 am and on a Saturday morning. I had even started to compose a harshly worded letter of complaint in my head when I realised the noise was actually Kamran and his brother snoring. It was impossible to say who was louder, but I categorically refused to sleep over again. Kamran claimed he had a cousin who was louder than him, and his cousin's family used ear protection at night. Back at the bank, when there was a water fight truce (I'll explain later), the toilet cubicles provided a haven for power nappers such as myself.

When another Asian male joined our department, the manager struggled with his name, which was Shahid, and decided that his new name would be Shaun, as it was the closest thing to his real name. It was when people could get away with a bit of casual racism. Due to Shahid being of very thin build at the time, the manager claimed, he brought new meaning to the term "skeleton staff."

In 1998, a graduate in Business Studies also joined us and claimed he would work there for a few weeks until something better came along. He insisted he was the only person in the post room who had a work ethic. He was wrong. I also had a work ethic. Mine just happened to be a poor one. When he was off, it meant the rest of us had to increase our output.

During one lunch break, as Kamran and I walked through the city centre, we came across someone we had been to school with. This chap would tell anyone who listened about how well he was doing and would almost certainly put us down. Legend has it that he once critiqued a free meal. Everything he uttered had to be taken with a lorry load of industrial salt. Kamran pleaded with me that under no circumstances should we admit to him we were dogsbodies. Kamran concocted a story he believed would make the other guy feel inadequate. A futile endeavour, I thought. Kamran explained to him he was the Correspondence Classifications and Extrications Manager at a bank, to which the guy didn't bat an eyelid. He carried on with such absurd self-importance that it was obvious he believed every word he spoke. This caused me to lose interest immediately, and I hadn't been paying attention for quite some time. He then asked what I was doing with my life, but I couldn't be bothered with the pact I'd made with Kamran.

"I'm an insignificant and meaningless cog in the system," I claimed, as dispassionately as noting that one of his nostrils was a different shape than the other one. They were vastly different shapes, a lot like the nostrils of the famous comedians, The Two Ronnies. Surprisingly, there wasn't any obvious hair looking to escape from his nose.

"That's not a job title though, is it?" He pointed out as he raised an eyebrow.

"I'm a letter opener at the same bank," I embarrassingly admitted. He appeared to be in shock and grimaced, "How on earth did someone like you get a job in a bank?"

"By applying," I replied, but my sarcasm was wasted on him.

"How does it feel that a £2 sharp metal object, otherwise known as a letter opener, does the same job as you?" He observed, and I sighed.

The man is a bona fide, card-carrying moron. Even his own mother would say that about him. Actually, I'm quoting her. He's the type of guy even the Salvation Army would put a hit on. I scrabbled desperately around in the deepest recesses of my mind for an appropriate response and countered with, "I've never thought of it that way." His reply to this was, "Let me make note of that in case I need to counter someone with rapier wit and articulacy." You don't want to know what I muttered under my cheese and onion pasty breath. That exchange was a microcosm of my entire existence. About two weeks later, I thought of a witty retort to the guy's insult. We haven't had a conversation since that day, but for many years I wanted to craftily weave my response to his insult into a conversation. The witty response couldn't have been that witty, as I now cannot recall it. He's the type of person who would write the foreword for his autobiography and sniff his own farts. Why he didn't give himself a double-barrelled surname also remains a mystery.

Despite his insults, I was content with what I had accomplished and didn't have the drive to better myself. My permanent residence was the slow lane of life, with occasional stops on the hard shoulder to get my bad breath back from the whizzing of the fast cars going past me or to give way to mobility scooters. It wasn't worth attempting to get into second gear because I would only get back into first gear moments later.

The work was unbelievably easy as we got it done by 9 am, even though our shift ended at 2 pm. Our location in the corner of a vast office was perfect to avoid detection from prying eyes. This meant that we would have a football quiz most days, which I always won due to my encyclopaedic knowledge.

While I sometimes had the potential to be lazy, Kamran was lazier, and Shahid lazier still. Some of the blame could be placed at my door as I had advised Shahid, on his first day, to be himself, and he took that literally. Just as he brought new meaning to the term "skeleton staff," he also brought new meaning to the term "casual worker." As I informed Shahid I would detail his laziness in the book, he dished out some industrial standard cursing before threatening me with legal action and illegal violence.

If Shahid and Kamran want to take legal action against me for these opinions, they are more than welcome. Firstly, they wouldn't know how to do it, and secondly, they know I'm right. The dossier I have on them is big enough to flatten a dinosaur. Shahid was lazy to a degree I felt was humanly impossible. Too lazy to even tell a running joke, not even one about Gary Lineker.

The manager didn't start until two hours after us, and Shahid was at least thirty minutes late every day, so much so that you could've set your watch by him. He really struggled with the notion of punctuality and even more with the notion of honest endeavour. About three hours into his shift, he would place a newspaper in a folder and retreat to the toilets for an hour. Kamran and I felt he had to be taught a tough life lesson for leaving us to do the work. Only one thing would unseat him from the toilet and make his time there one of fear and paranoia. This is how the water fights started. What follows might seem childish, but for those involved, it was deadly serious. Kamran and I followed Shahid into the toilets, and we launched wet paper towels into his cubicle. We had planned to throw a lot more at him, but other people were using the toilets, and we had to flee. When Shahid returned, he declared war on us. We agreed on one simple rule, which was that the person had to be in a toilet cubicle to be a legitimate target. We spent more time plotting and carrying out the water fights than actually working. It was each man for himself, but there were occasional short-lived alliances, which ultimately led to double crosses.

Every day was like a game of hide and seek when using the toilets. It was a free-for-all between the three of us and led to many minor skirmishes. Many a time, I waited until I got home to use the toilet. Kamran and I decided that enough was enough, and we had to join forces.

As Shahid left with his newspaper in a folder, we waited for a few minutes and began military-style searches/sweeps of all the floors. On the virtually deserted seventh floor, we discovered a locked cubicle and a pair of feet inside. In something straight out of Mission Impossible, I placed an 'OUT OF ORDER' sign on the outside of the main door.

We used paper towels and water balloons. My coup de grâce was a large water rifle that had also previously been filled with water to avoid wasting any time. While this was going on, we could hear the sounds of flatulence and squirting. He was ready for the taking and couldn't come out of the cubicle. We went over, under, and with insults hurled at him, too. At one point, I fell to the floor, like James Bond, and shot at his legs. He disguised his voice and asked who we were and what we wanted. We weren't stupid enough to fall for the oldest and most obvious trick. It probably lasted about a minute, but it was relentless. It was just like Call of Duty but was real and for grown-ups.

As we returned to the post room, we sat together, chuckling at our handiwork. Shahid then returned but was as dry as a Taliban wedding. It perplexed us about what had just transpired. "Where have you been?"

"Toilet,"

"Which one?"

"Disabled one on ground floor," he smiled.

"Well, that's an outrageous violation of the niceties of battle," I insisted. We'd been out-foxed by the laziest man I'd ever seen. That's a whole different level of ignominy.

Who was the mystery person with bowel problems? Surely it wasn't Lineker, was it? It will forever remain a mystery. A lot like the true identity of DB Cooper, how fluff ends up in bellybuttons, or how Julia Roberts was cast in the film *Pretty Woman* instead of an actual pretty woman. We never got to the bottom of it. The water fights ended because the disabled toilets (that's what we called them at the time, for those who disapprove of the description) were virtually impenetrable. It all simply fizzled out. Years later, when Shahid asked to use the toilet at my house, the powerful urge for vengeance came over me. The water wars had never officially ended, and he was still a legitimate target. It was also debatable whether the toilet constituted a cubicle, as per the rules. Any attack would have meant making up a phenomenally good excuse for my wife for why the bathroom had been flooded and why the kitchen ceiling was leaking. There is some sort of moral or allegorical meaning to this, but I can't for the life of me work out what it is.

When the early starts became too much for Kamran, he proclaimed he didn't wish to be an unskilled post opener for the remainder of his working life, because it was 'creatively unrewarding.' The most surprising thing was that he could put those two words together. This led to his transfer to the General and Banking Department, where the cheques were processed. Just like in a TV show, he was like an actor who assumed he could make it in films, a lot like the cast of Friends. Even though General and Banking were in the next room, they didn't have the laid-back attitude of the post room; they had stringent policies and were shockingly figure-driven. If the post room was a holiday camp, this was a concentration camp. The boss even shared his birthday with Adolf Hitler. Kamran now worked the 08.00-16.00 shift instead of the 06.00-14.00 shift, the post room worked. As Shahid and I finished at 2 pm, we waved goodbye at an obviously distressed Kamran in a condescending manner. He only lasted a week, which was still four days more than anybody had predicted. This was still a lot longer than I would have done in such a measured environment. Staff from the departments other than the post room seemed to have been hypnotised by banking rhetoric and jargon, which bred blatant careerism.

In 1995, I also had loftier aspirations and applied for my dream job but failed because of the poor vision in my right eye, which could possibly be tracked back to the small black and white television. I shrugged off the disappointment and lackadaisically carried on as a poorly paid but happy menial worker. Who was I kidding? I didn't really expect to get the job but felt it was worth trying my luck. It would have been a miracle if it had happened.

One man who had been successful in achieving his dream job was a man known as Big Jim. He was a retired Police Officer but was now just a Danka. The only qualification he claimed to possess was a PhD in Common Sense from the University of Life. His language was as blue as his old uniform, and he practically used a swear word before every noun. As a uniformed patrol officer, he had worked on the Ripper enquiry, but only to preserve the integrity of crime scenes. Knowing Big Jim as I do, he probably fell asleep moments after getting there.

My first recollection of the Ripper was my mum trying to scare me into going inside for bedtime; otherwise, I'd be his latest victim. It did the trick as I fully experienced the climate of fear that was prevalent in Northern England at the time. For a while, I thought he was coming after me personally. Apart from possibly the children of the Ripper's victims, I was the child most scared of him. He seemed like a shadowy, supernatural figure who would kill and then disappear into the abyss. It was massive news when he was finally caught in 1981. By that time, thirteen lives had been lost, and those who survived would never be the same again. Although I was too young to recall, one of his victims was discovered only about 500 metres from where we lived at the time. His house was also only a dangerously close 1.3 miles from ours. Forty years later, he still casts a giant shadow over the city.

Big Jim had spent his entire career in uniform because he didn't have any ambition beyond that. I was expecting to hear about his heroics, but he claimed he spent most of his time trying to dodge work. Instead of being fastidious and austere, as you'd expect from a former Police Officer, he was unashamedly slapdash. His belief was that any acts of heroism in the police meant there would be innumerable forms to fill in afterwards. Apparently, it created an extremely time-consuming and expensive process known as an investigation. He avoided investigations like a lazy man would avoid hard work. That's the best simile I can think of. He waged a one-man war, not on crime or criminals but against crime numbers and red tape. The biggest (and probably only successful) investigations of his career (by his own admission) had been to track down the person responsible for accidentally damaging his mug at the station, those who had informed his superiors of his exploits, or anyone who had eaten his sandwiches. There was never any danger of him becoming a Private Investigator after he'd retired from the police. If only his attention to detail was as good as his attention to kebabs.

Big Jim claimed to only work at the bank for beer money, as he already had an ample police pension. Judging by his beer belly, he was getting paid a lot more than the rest of us or knew of an inexpensive beer place. He had the standard spongy purple nose to go with his belly. Although he never referred to it as a belly, more like an alcohol storage facility. To him, beer wasn't a problem; it was the solution. His war now was against liver disease, diabetes, and blood pressure. The only fitness goal he had was to be able to walk to the nearest pub, or even crawl if he had to. You wouldn't find many human beings in greater need of diversity courses and diet plans. It is bizarre how your expectations change. As a teenager, I wanted to be like Des Walker, a world-class football player. As I got older, my heroes were the likes of Big Jim, and he became my mentor. I was now more impressed with people who could work out efficient working practices, which should definitely not be confused with laziness.

A Big Danka named Terry Walker (no relation of Des) was in almost as much need of diversity courses. He was the least lazy Big Danka (which isn't saying much) and was lung achingly funny. He described himself as a man of great social and political conscience, but nobody else did. On one occasion, he was the only Big Danka in the office and sat at their sorting table as their phone rang. He carried on munching on his sandwich as though he was deaf or invisible. The manager marched over to him in a rage and hollered, "Answer the bloody phone." The manager was a rotund bulldog of a woman, which was ironically her nickname. Bulldog, that is. It wouldn't have been much of a nickname if it were longer than her actual name. She looked like the pretty one from the Australian prison drama *Prisoner Cell Block H*. Yes, I knew there wasn't an actual pretty one. She was as unenthusiastic a leader as you could find and perfectly suited to the role. Her financial management skills were legendary. She didn't just watch her pennies but put them under 24-hour surveillance. To her, spending a penny was splashing out.

Back at the office, the phone stopped ringing but then started again. Terry remained calm and carried on chewing. The whole post room fell silent, and the only thing that could be heard was the phone. All eyes were fixated on Terry and the manager. We were like the crowd at a tennis tournament, and our heads darted from side to side, and by the end, we were all ready to be hypnotised. Terry knew he was the centre of attention and didn't care. It was the most outward act of defiance I had ever witnessed.

He swallowed his food and wiped his mouth. After a sharp intake of breath, he addressed the post room like the captain of a naval ship preparing his troops for war. "I'm on my lunch break. There will be some changes around here from now on." He didn't have to say anything more and did not even quote any employment legislation to justify his actions or inactions on this occasion. The silence had reached deafening proportions, and you could have heard a feather drop. The manager shook her head in admonition while she released a lengthy and loud moan. Terry carried on eating, and the phone kept on ringing. He deserved a rousing ovation, and if I had a hat, I'd have taken it off to him. He wasn't just a man's man; he was a man's, man's man. Terry was correct, and the incident was a catalyst for some change at Danka. The incident caught the attention of the senior management, who brought about wholesale changes around meal times. The meal times were now staggered so that there was always someone to answer the phone. The consumption of food was no longer permitted in the office either. They weren't the changes Terry was expecting. Few adhered to these new policies, and after a few weeks, we reverted to the old ways.

Terry Walker had a younger sidekick, and the two of them had charmed the old dears at the canteen at a smaller sorting centre into giving them massive free sandwiches. They would collect these as they delivered and collected post. They were something out of a black and white Peter Sellers film and knew every trick.

Terry later contracted cancer and would joke about wanting 'Staying Alive' played at his funeral. Terry, Kamran, Shahid, and I would frequently go out for curries, even after Terry had retired as a Danka, He was renowned for his generosity, and he often attempted to pay for all of us. He wouldn't have just given you the shirt off his back but would have let you borrow his only pair of underpants, even if later that day he was entering a hot curry eating contest in his thinnest white trousers. When his condition worsened, we would meet him at his house. On my last visit, his wife took me to one side and revealed that the doctors hadn't given him much time. She was understandably in tears. By this time, he was in a wheelchair and unable to walk. He was a well-groomed man, even in his sixties. He would gel his hair back, and his beard line was always exquisitely neat. There wasn't even a sniff of protruding nasal hair. It was tragic to watch his health deteriorate and to see him in pain. He had a firm faith in God and an afterlife, which provided him with strength. I visited him on a Saturday and advised him I would return a week later with a homemade curry for him. As I left, I told him I loved him and looked forward to seeing him a week later.

He passed away a few days later before I could get the curry to him. He was marvellous company and was a perennial source of joy to anyone who ever met him. I still miss him. The memorial service was a jolly affair, and the vicar could have been a good stand-up comedian in his spare time, as he spent much of the proceedings making fun of Terry's poor son-in-law. He didn't break into a karaoke version of Staying Alive, as I was half expecting.

It was all light-hearted, and everyone seemed

happy. It's not relevant, but I was the only Asian person present, apart from demonstrating how open-minded and culturally diverse I am. This now sounds like a civil service job application where I have to present examples of my respect for race and diversity. It paints me as a beacon of integration and multi-culturalism if nothing else. After I left Danka, a company named Pitney Bowes took them over, but nobody referred to the Big Dankas as Big Pitney Bowes. It didn't have the same highly inappropriate ring to it. Looking back now, I enjoyed every minute of my time as a Baby Danka, and it was partly due to one of the most obvious reasons of all, I was still young. It was the happiest time of my life up to that point.

THE CHAPTER ABOUT HOW I TRY TO MEET DES WALKER

The England manager resigned after the failure to qualify for the 1994 World Cup. Subsequent managers failed to select Des for the England team again, even though his performances for his club side were still flawless. So my interest in football went into sharp decline. There had seldom been a greater fall from grace in football in such a short space of time. He'd gone from England's first-choice defender to being discarded. My support for the England national team had shifted into dislike. Most would assume this dislike was for ideological reasons, such as race, religion, colonisation, discrimination, integration, or immigration. However, it was actually because of Des Walker. It's not worth my time to explain the long, boring story. One way around it could be that I keep a copy of this boring book handy and give it out whenever someone asks.

In 1999, an opportunity presented itself to somehow meet Des Walker when his team came to my hometown to play against Bradford City. I had the whole summer to plan this meeting and decided to write a heartfelt letter to him. I explained why he meant so much to me and why I thought he was so badly mistreated by the England national team. Not too dissimilar to this book, I suppose. It was addressed to Des Walker at his club stadium. My imagination ran wild about how Des Walker would read my letter and write a detailed response where he acknowledged my loyalty. A couple of weeks later, I received a generic letter from the club, thanking me for my support and a team photograph. It was the equivalent of a modern-day 'out of office' email. Looking back now, what else did I expect from the letter? They were probably laughing at my naivety.

On the day of the game, I packed my pockets with industrial strength mints and got ready to meet my hero. The best way to meet him, I had been advised by a steward, was to loiter near the players' entrance after the game. This way, I could briefly catch his attention as he boarded the coach on his way back home. There was some apprehension on my part as I had heard rumours for many years about his aloofness with fans.

The only other celebrity (C-level, admittedly) I'd ever met prior to that was TV presenter Rav Wilding, and that hadn't ended well. That meeting happened at my workplace, as we washed our hands at wash basins next to each other in the toilets. He remarked how cold it was, and I inquired whether he meant in the toilets or in Leeds. His response was a very straight forward and serious, "Leeds." There appeared to be some real chemistry between us. As I was about to propose that we should form a career as a comedy double act, he walked away before I could say another word. The brief exchange is probably etched in his consciousness. My bog-standard toilet humour might have been too risqué for a clean-cut performer like him, but we would never know for certain.

Des had an amazing game that day, as he always did. Afterwards, I made my way to the players' entrance. As Des emerged, he was swarmed by fans and started to sign autographs. As long as I didn't demonstrate some world-class level of idiocy, I would be safe. "Did you read my letter?" I asked earnestly. Thinking back now, the nervousness must have caused all common sense to escape from my body. How would he have read it if they'd sent me a generic reply from an admin assistant, secretary, or some snotty-nosed trainee? The letter wouldn't have got anywhere near him. The other people present started staring at me like I was a nincompoop, and they were right. He gave me the response my stupid question warranted. "Which letter? Do you think I read every letter?" What I said next was probably more incoherent babble. A couple of people started sniggering. Others had a look of bewilderment. This was developing into a Mr Bean level of embarrassing now. What was probably seconds seemed like palaeolithic eons. I tried to conceal my disappointment and compose myself but failed miserably. My ability to get things wrong and totally misconstrue the situation is unparalleled. I'm actually cringing and screwing my face up with embarrassment as I write. To avoid any further indignity, I had to get away because the damage was irreversible. Mathematics was never my strong point, but I would suggest it was an embarrassing moment number 2,745,623 of my life, or in that region anyway. Unfortunately, it doesn't blur in with a myriad of similar embarrassing encounters. This one was different and would rankle me for a long time. At that moment, I suffered the greatest humiliation in human history, apart from perhaps any former celebrity who couldn't make it through the application stage of Celebrity Big Brother.

Never meet your heroes, especially if you've got the potential for your brain to turn to mush when you meet the said hero. If someone had asked me how life was treating me, I would have retorted, "Like I had run over its cat or hadn't liked its dog photos on social media." The story appeared to have ended that day with a big, fat full stop. Any continuation seemed as likely as someone with a face tattoo having a successful job interview. Some soul-searching questions were asked of myself. Here I was, a grown man, still hero-worshipping a footballer from my youth. Maybe I was desperately trying to cling to my youth. He would always be a part of my childhood, but childhood fandom should not end this way. All those years I watched him, read about him, and talked about him seemed like a complete waste of time. There were so many highs and lows we'd been through together. All that meant nothing now. This isn't the fairy tale ending from the films or books I was expecting and so badly craved. I hadn't helped myself with the stupid question, but that wasn't the response I was expecting. In my head, I was still making excuses for him and myself. The long-standing rumours about his relationship with fans might actually be true. It simply wasn't fair for it to end this way. By this stage, a lot of you will be screaming at the page with something like (and rightly so), "Forget Des Walker now and get on with your life, you saddo." My mate wasn't only thinking about it but shouted it loudly. As time went on, Des became less newsworthy than ever, but I would still check for any happenings, significant or otherwise, in the life of Des Walker. Nothing in football could replace the unmitigated joy of watching Des Walker play. Therefore, football was banished from my life. It was sent into exile, like the family of a former dictator.

LOCK, STOCK, AND ONE SMOKING METAL ROLLING PIN.

The names and locations have been changed for this chapter to protect the innocent and the guilty because I don't have a strong enough legal team or a death wish. While Des' career was winding down, my life was in mortal danger. The second part of that sentence was something I never expected to use. It all started with what I still acknowledge to be one of the biggest mistakes of my life. In late 2001, my dad first suggested I should try to better myself and that he knew of someone who was selling a pizza shop in another town. With a hard heart and a lump in my throat, I said goodbye to the world of Danka. I wished I had the guts to tell him that menial work was about as much as I was capable of. Before I knew it, I was self-employed in the catering industry. I shadowed the old owner for a few weeks and was then left to run it. From the outset, it was an undoubted calamity, in every sense apart from financially. The stress was greater than anything I had ever known, which was in complete contrast to my life as a Danka. The days would come and go with monotonous regularity. For the first six months, I didn't have a single day off and was away from home for approximately twelve hours a day. It was hard, strenuous work, as well as being physically and emotionally draining. I was in a constant state of exhaustion, and the long hours were taking a toll on my mental health. It's the closest I've ever come to being depressed, but my faith helped me to battle through it. The whole family was relying on the shop, and we had paid a lot of money for it. It wasn't easy to simply sell up and leave. I also kept telling myself it had real potential.

The place was a magnet for drunken morons from the nearby pub. I might as well have put up a massive neon sign stating, "This establishment particularly welcomes patronage from drunken morons and huge discounts offered for any racism thrown in." The only real benefit of keeping it was I could devour as much junk food and drink as much fizzy pop as my heart desired, which was a lot. I was way ahead of the game because, in 2002, my diet was precisely the same as a typical British ten-year-old in 2021. Despite my utter disregard for my body mass index or the state of my heart, my weight remained at a constant nine stone and six pounds.

A few weeks after taking over the pizza shop, a highly intoxicated male walked into the shop. Well, I say walk, but it was more of a stumble. He was carrying a polystyrene food container in one hand and used the other hand to maintain his balance on the wall as he came in. His odour was a blend of White Lightning cider and Gary Lineker's shorts from the 1990 World Cup game against Ireland. His smell arrived a few seconds before he did. Credit where credit is due, I never suffered from a blocked nose again. His attire suggested he was an inhabitant of shop doorways or was hard of living arrangements. He tried to hand me the partially open polystyrene box and urged me to warm it up for him. When I quizzed him about where he had found the box, he nonchalantly responded, "In the bin outside." The box contained chips, but I could see movement inside. As I drew closer, I saw many slugs living amongst the chips. I have a terrible gag reflex and started gipping uncontrollably as my stomach churned. The ghastly sight had caused me to buckle as if a giant, world boxing champion octopus had punched me repeatedly in the stomach. I was gasping for air. The male gave me a perplexed look and shuffled back out, using his distinct holding-the-wall technique. He then huddled under the brightly lit lamppost to examine the box. It's probable that his taste buds, if he had any left, would have struggled to differentiate between a warm slug and a cold chip. He may even have mistaken the slugs for freshly made Jelly Baby sweets. Goodness only knows how that story concluded because I was too busy on the toilet, trying not to vomit. This man was a walking advertisement for the dangers of alcoholism.

It pretty much put me off food for two days, and even then, I had to make a phased return. There's no reason to include this story apart from wishing that you are squirming with revulsion, which is precisely how I feel as I write.

If it wasn't the drunks and their slugs, it was the Environmental Health people. There wasn't enough time for anything else, and I, therefore, didn't have any social life. The money was better than Danka but not sufficient to make it worth my while. There was also the issue of machinery breaking down when the timer for the pizza oven burnt out and the oven stopped functioning. In the days before smart phones, I used the Yellow Pages book to find a commercial electrician. The one selected arrived two hours late and charged me £90 for merely turning up and fixing it in the short term, but wanted £350 to fix it permanently. I wasn't sure if I had misread the Yellow Pages and had called a commercial fraudster instead. When I asked him if he was being serious, he claimed that with it being a Sunday, I was lucky to be only paying that much. The only thing lucky about it was that I wasn't a vulnerable, elderly person with dementia, in which case he would have charged double. He took out the burnt-out timer and advised me to get a new one. He temporarily fixed the problem within 15 minutes. I sarcastically thanked him and told him not to darken my door again. The next day, I purchased a replacement part for £67, and a customer's friend installed it in ten minutes for £20 and a pizza.

The incident provided me with the incentive to enrol myself on a part-time electrical installation course, as it could also offer my route out of the food industry. This enrolment was surprising to many people, because I didn't even know how to wire a plug prior to that. I managed to convince my mate Kamran to start the course with me, but he quit after a week. The reason he quit, sums him up more than anything he's ever said or done. His exact words were, "what's the point in me doing the course, when I know if you do the course, you're gonna do all the work at my house for free anyway?"

The course was a struggle, and I was close to quitting myself, after a few weeks, but a fellow student named Steve, offered me some encouragement. He asked me what I thought of the course, and I told him I was going to quit because I was rubbish. He advised me to stay so that we could both be rubbish together. Steve and I were the only ones on the course who didn't have any previous experience in the construction industry. We were both equally lacking in confidence. Another student named Dan was the opposite of us in the confidence stakes and took me under his wing. Eventually, it started to make sense, and after a few months, I did what any lazy person would do; I installed a light switch next to my bed so that I wouldn't have to get up to switch the light off. For someone who had never fixed anything, it was a eureka moment. It showed that I had a greater capacity to learn than I had given myself credit for. Dan is now a leading authority on lights, and Steve is a self-employed electrician who has more work than he can handle. I am still in contact with both of them and won't forget how much they encouraged me.

In November 2020, Steve sent me a message stating he had done some electrical work at The Yorkshire Ripper's old house, and astonishingly, his ex-wife Sonia still lived there. She was now married to a hairdresser, and one newspaper had described this union as, "Sonia Sutcliffe marries The Yorkshire Snipper." Although, Steve claimed he would have gone for the more obvious 'Yorkshire Clipper.' Steve joked that he'd made sure he kept his hammer close to himself. I had to remind him there wasn't any indication that Sonia had any history of attacking people with hammers, unlike her ex-husband. My legal team has instructed me to be mindful of what I write because Sonia has a history of taking legal action. Some of her victims include the magazine Private Eye and newspapers Daily Express, Daily Star, and the News of the World. If she is contemplating taking legal action against me, I would like to point her toward Steve. They can sort it out between themselves, and she already has his mobile number. Sonia wanted to replace a socket in her kitchen and told him from the outset there wasn't any cash in the house. Steve assumed this to be a warning in case he had any thoughts of stealing from her. She closed all the doors, so he wasn't allowed to see any part of the house apart from the kitchen, where he was forced to work with live wires. Her house, and particularly the household appliances, didn't look as if they had been changed since her infamous ex-husband lived there. To add to Steve's woes, she asked him to drive her to the cash machine after the work had been completed. As soon as she handed him the money, he drove off and left her to walk home. Just like her ex-husband's victims, Steve claimed he wanted her to experience the dread of walking alone on a cold winter's night in a Northern English city. All this while a Bradfordian with a bushy beard and unkempt hair (due to barber shops being closed because of the Covid-19 lockdown rather than a style choice), who was supremely adept at handling a hammer, was driving about in a rage. Only those familiar with the Ripper's appearance and sickening methods of attack would fully appreciate what Steve meant. In a strange and chilling coincidence, two days after this communication, the Ripper died in prison.

What was also coincidental in 2005 was my chance encounter with retired Police Officer Andrew Laptew. This was the man who had identified Peter Sutcliffe as the Ripper two years before he was apprehended. Laptew's bosses had ignored him because they were convinced a hoaxer from the North East was the actual Ripper. The hoaxer had sent letters and a tape recording claiming he was the Yorkshire Ripper. Ironically, the hoaxer had been arrested a couple of weeks before I met

Laptew, and it was because of DNA he had left on one of the envelopes he had sent almost thirty years earlier. Laptew now worked for the police in a civilian capacity as a Financial Investigator and was having a meal with some work colleagues. We discussed the recent arrest of the hoaxer, and Laptew said it was strange how things worked out sometimes. There was a lot more I wanted to ask him about the Ripper case, but he was busy, and I didn't want to annoy him any more than I had already.

While at the shop, I got talking to a customer who worked in the profession I had unsuccessfully applied for in 1995. I mentioned to him I had previously failed at the medical stage of the recruitment process because of my poor sight in one eye, and he claimed they had now lowered the eyesight standards. He encouraged me to apply again, and that was precisely what I did. The application form seemed far more complicated than ten years previously. It was more complex than an accountant's expense forms and thicker than a list of Jeremy Clarkson's inappropriate comments. It would have been easy for me to give up as usual, but I didn't.

One of the most worrying parts of the application was the one regarding the required body mass index. At 5'10" tall and nine stone, six pounds, I was underweight. This required me to do something I'd never done before, which was to lift weights, because shrinking to 5'5" wasn't really an option. A combination of weights and gorging on fast food finally got me up to the required weight. By some strange miracle, or as I like to believe, divine intervention, I passed all the aptitude and physical tests. The pass mark for the aptitude tests was 50%, and I achieved 54%. I achieved it by a whisker, or as you'd expect me to say, by a nasal hair. The only thing remaining was a background check for criminal convictions, and I knew this would come back cleaner than a monk's underwear. As I was waiting, I had the misfortune of becoming mixed up with some unsavoury characters.

On one busy Friday night, the shop door flew open, and the metallic handle struck the tiled wall, which caused a loud bang. It was an act that Shakespeare fans might call foreshadowing. The events of that day will always remain firmly embedded in my brain. A male, who I will refer to as Damian, stormed into the shop with two people, who I will refer to as his goons. He made the type of entrance you typically see in films when the police break the door down to catch drug dealers by surprise. He was a man of imposing proportions and almost filled the door. As he stormed in, he aggressively looked at me and yelled, "Oi muppet, call me a taxi now." It didn't take long to attain a balanced and well-informed opinion of Damian. His actions were consistent with someone whom experts in human behaviour would describe as 'a certified moron.' With a deep sigh, I walked towards the landline phone because I felt if I complied, he would get into his taxi and leave. He looked at me with utter contempt, like I was something his neighbour's dog had deposited on the business end of his freshly purchased barbeque. I asked him what his name was, as the taxi firms do when taking a booking. He gave me his name and told me to get on with it. Due to it being a hectic Friday night, the earliest they could get there was in an hour, which infuriated Damian further. As he spoke, his nostrils flared with rage. It was difficult to establish where his thick, nasal hair ended and where his colossal moustache started. If his moustache was anything to go by, his other life choices needed to be seriously questioned. It was as though it had been hand-woven into a single entity. At first, I thought it was an optical illusion. He seemed to be oblivious to it all, even though it was going on right under his nose. The only thing separating us was the small length of worktop, and before I could recommend the Ryobi 18V cordless brand of chainsaw to trim his nasal hair, he gripped my arm tightly and wouldn't let go. We were now close enough for me to be almost intoxicated and knocked out by his breath alone. His breath appeared to be a mixture of stodgy, bitter beer and Satan's farts. If he had opened his mouth slightly wider, I'd probably have seen the tail of a dead rat hanging down. He exclaimed I was a 'dog' and, in the process, sprayed my face with his saliva. I made a mental note to myself to contact my GP in case I needed some type of rabies vaccine or some medication for rodenticide toxicity.

The situation was escalating rapidly, and I was becoming increasingly apprehensive. I pulled my arm away, eventually. He then looked at his goons for acknowledgement and let out a maniacal laugh. They chuckled fiendishly and looked approvingly back at him. It was as though he was performing on stage for his goons while I was his stooge. The goons had the obligatory earrings, tracksuits tucked into their socks, cigarettes in their hands; the only thing they lacked were 'chav' tattoos on their foreheads. They were the sort of people, if you saw them wearing buttoned shirts, you'd shout, "good luck in court."

There wasn't much I could do but politely ask him to leave. Even though I knew it was unlikely to work and it didn't. He then banged on the worktop with the bottom of his fist, which generated enough pressure to cause the glass panel underneath to shatter. There were a couple of customers in the shop, and they must have been rightly worried for their safety because they ran outside.

I then walked around to where he was standing to check the full extent of the damage. He looked at me with complete disdain and shouted, "What are you gonna do, what you gonna do?" What could I do, apart from roll my eyes with exasperation and curse him under my garlicky kebab breath? Not even the cunning and guile of a BBC television licence enforcement officer would be sufficient to get rid of him.

I was a man without confidence in my ability to fight, and a lot of it was because of my size. Inwardly, I was seething with rage. It was the most worthless, helpless, and unmanly I had ever felt in my life. It wasn't something you'd wish on double-glazing salespeople, payday loan company bosses, or those who set the prices for cinema food. I told him he was right because there was nothing I could do and asked him again to leave. He wouldn't know common decency if it lived next door to him for ten years and regularly exchanged birthday cards.

My dad was at the back somewhere and asked what was happening. As described before, he was a man who had never backed down from a fight. He ignored my pleas to stay at the back and went out to investigate at the front of the shop. As my dad surveyed the damage to the counter, Damian moved closer and tried to headbutt him. The war horn had been sounded, and for maximum effect, the War theme from Rocky 4 here should be played now. My dad moved out of the way and slapped him on the face. Damian was incensed and grabbed a metal rolling pin, which was within reach of where he was standing. It was completely useless at rolling dough and had been carelessly left within reach of any customer. He took hold of it with what clearly appeared to be sinister intentions. This led to an almighty struggle for the rolling pin between all of us. I had to summon up every morsel of strength from my weak body to take the weapon from him. It seemed like an out-of-body experience. Against the odds, we dispossessed him, and somehow, I was one with the rolling pin in my hand. His two goons weren't laughing anymore and ran out. Because of my UFC fandom, I will now bombard you with references to the sport of mixed martial arts. I had to include them somehow, and this was the perfect opportunity. Damian had a significant weight advantage against me, even if I was weighed with the rolling pin. The rolling pin would give me a ridiculously unfair reach advantage though, which nullified his weight advantage. I still maintain that he would have failed any post-fight drug tests if it were a sanctioned fight.

Damian moved closer to me, and I was in fear for my life. There were virtually nanoseconds to react. My thoughts went back to Miss Watson's GCSE Physics class to work out the newtons of force required to incapacitate this monster of a man. Don't ever let anyone tell you physics and maths aren't useful in the real world. I was around a metre away, and the metal rolling pin was approximately 5kg. F=ma, acceleration is d, divided by time squared, and this wasn't a straight line. Would I need to calculate the distance travelled using Pi x radius? What about the centripetal force? Not to mention the metal composition of the rolling pin, the thickness of the greasy air in the shop, and the bone density of his skull. Were my assessments even correct? Because my life was in mortal peril, my survival instincts took over. With gritted teeth, like that of a heavily constipated man, but with the desperation of someone with severe diarrhoea and outright disregard for the manufacturer's instructions and equations, I simply struck him as hard as I could.

With a metallic thud, the handle slammed into the top of his head. As the handle made contact, it broke and flew backwards, straight back over my head.

My precision was like that of a surgeon while almost certainly creating work for a surgeon or two. Don't even ask where I stood with the warranty of the rolling pin. It may have been ineffective for rolling dough, but in the self-defence department, it was a cast iron hit. Damian was struck only once, and his cries for help were almost deafening. The force of the strike was sufficient to cause thick, green, and spongy snot (as well as some hair, I imagine) to fire out of one or both of his nostrils like a ball from a cannon. The speed with which it flew out made it difficult for the naked eye to establish if it was two balls of snot that had merged into one or if it was indeed a solitary ball from a solitary nostril. It was a time before smartphones, and if it had happened now, it would have been filmed by someone from a bedroom. The slow-motion feature might have solved that particular conundrum. It might have even gone viral and made Damian a social media sensation. Irrespective of how many nostrils the snot flew out from, it must have cleared the way for air to finally pass through his nose. It would have been hard for him to wrap his head around what had just happened. The force I used that day was reasonable, lawful, and proportionate. For clarification, Section 3 of the Criminal Law Act 1967 states, "A person may use such force as is reasonable in the prevention of crime." My swift actions had certainly prevented a multitude of offences.

Just as you have my blood, sweat, tears, and brain matter in your hands, I had Damian's in my hands, virtually glued to the rolling pin. A strange sense of peace and tranquillity came over me. Similar to sitting under the pleasant shade of a Mulberry tree, on the soft green grass next to a stream of clear, flowing water on a warm summer evening. All this while, I breathed in the fresh aroma of freshly cut grass and ate low-hanging mulberries as birds chirped and cows grazed in a nearby field.

As I was daydreaming, Damian's breath woke me up and brought me back to reality. The look on his face suggested his spirit was crushed, and his demise was in full swing. As we were to find out later, others had suffered at his hands, and there would undoubtedly have been many more. My dad, in his typically understated fashion, then said something which I can best translate as, "He's been suitably advised about his impropriety," and waved off the contest like a UFC referee. When it was over, we handed over a barely conscious Damian to his two goons (cornermen) like a baton in a sprint relay. Damian wasn't in any fit state to understand, but I felt I had to remind him of our policies on threatening behaviour towards the staff, "Consider yourself barred for life, you dog, and so are your goons." His injury needed an appropriate insult, and it was only fair, it should be his own insult. If I had some salt to hand, I would have rubbed it into his head too. It was unlikely he could recall his own name, never mind trespass policies. His cronies were struggling to lift him by the arms, as he was much bigger than them.

My dad then offered his medical prognosis with the confidence of a world-renowned neurologist, "He'll easily walk that off." It made my fight record a respectable two wins and zero losses. Both fights had been against habitual bullies. As I was about to do a victory lap of honour, a taxi vehicle slowly drove next to the shop and stopped outside. The front passenger was a large black male, and so were the two passengers behind him. They didn't look familiar and were peering intently at Damian and myself. This is beginning to sound like a police statement. It became a three-way stare-down, like a scene from a spaghetti western between me, the men in the car, and Damian's two goons. It was an agonising silence, and our expressions portrayed the look of complete bewilderment you would normally associate with someone who'd met a drug addict with teeth.

The front passenger window of the car went down, and the driver, who was an Asian male in his fifties, leaned forward to make eye contact with me. He then shouted that he'd been looking for this rascal for the last three hours. He said this in Punjabi as he pointed to Damian, who was now being carried away by the arms. Although he didn't use the word rascal but used a derogatory Punjabi colloquialism, which a BBC newsreader would probably describe as Damian having an unusually close relationship with his own mother. The driver's language was more colourful than a rainbow, and if the said BBC newsreader interviewed him, the most common sound would have been a bleep. It appeared as though it wasn't the first or last time he'd set off on an expletive-laden expedition into the terrain of red mist. As I moved closer to the car, I saw that the male in the front passenger seat was carrying a bin liner that contained some type of long weapon. It was difficult to say what he had in the bin liner, but if it was a rolling pin, it was much bigger than mine. The driver explained he had been waiting for a customer, and Damian had forced his way into his taxi. Damian had become aggressive and refused to leave. It sounded all too familiar. The taxi driver had then been made to drive to the area of my shop under duress.

During the journey, Damian punched the driver on the back of the head and damaged his vehicle by kicking it as he left. The taxi driver had been consumed by the idea of revenge and had summoned his helpers to exact it. He shook his head and claimed Damian had been lucky he'd met us because if he'd met the boys in the car, he'd have also met his maker moments later. If you're already sick of my puns, you can have some more because he had a stroke of luck by meeting us. There was absolutely no doubt in my mind that my rolling pin and I had saved Damian's life, although he definitely wouldn't have appreciated it. The male in the front passenger side, who appeared to be the leader, then turned to the taxi driver and said, "Let's get out of here. We can't do much more to him. Police will be here soon, anyway." The driver assured me he'd return after dropping his boys off. He returned an hour later and claimed to have tracked Damian to a local hospital because of a contact he had there.

My concern now was whether there would be any police intervention if his injuries were severe, especially as I had never had any dealings with the police and did not know what to expect. Would I be the victim of a miscarriage of justice, like Stefan Kiszko, who wrongly spent 16 years in prison? Would I be sharing a cell with Big Bubba from Mississippi, who had somehow found his way into the British prison system? My mind was filled with paranoid thoughts. The taxi driver seemed too well-connected for someone in his profession. He then told me about how he had become acquainted with the boys in the car. They were members of an organised crime group and had used his taxi to transport them to a location for a business venture. By remaining quiet about the incident, he had bought their loyalty.

Later that day, a customer asked me if we had beaten someone up with frying pans. The place must have been rife with rumour and gossip about the earlier incident. We fixed the broken glass counter the next day while the blood and possible brain tissue were wiped off the walls straight away. Judging by the sound his head made, there wasn't much brain on offer. Some of you might describe this as a hollow victory. It wasn't the type of crime scene preservation Columbo would have approved of, and by this time, we didn't expect any police involvement, anyway. That should have been the end of the story.

The following Friday, someone from the nearby pub began to throw glass bottles at our delivery car. It wasn't difficult to work out why this was happening. Thankfully, none of it caused any damage, but it was unsettling. It was difficult to tell who the perpetrators were because of the angle of the pub entrance. With much trepidation, I left to investigate in the pub while trying to do my best to look inconspicuous. My suspicions were confirmed as soon as I walked in that the bottle-throwing was unmistakably a consequence of my dealings with Damian. Three males at the other end of the pub were staring intently at me. It wasn't difficult to gauge their intentions. One of the males looked menacingly at me and asked the other two, "Shall I beat him up now?" His eyes were firmly transfixed on me like a target. His bulging and veiny biceps could clearly be seen. He looked like the type of man you wouldn't wish to meet in a secluded dark alley, or ever really. During this story, I will refer to this male as Tim. With as much nonchalance as I could summon, I made my way to the exit. As I retreated to the relative safety of my shop, I received a phone call from Kamran. From the corner of my eye, I saw Tim walk into the shop, and thankfully, there was a worktop separating us. It was unlikely his visit was of a social or culinary nature. I quickly decided that I had to act tough, but Kamran was oblivious to what was happening.

"We are fully tooled up and ready for anything a muppet like Damian and his cronies can do," I tried to give the impression I wasn't aware of Tim's presence.

Kamran: "Who, what?"

Me: "Exactly, this isn't going to end well."

Kamran: "Eh?"

Tim then interjected angrily, "I know what you're talking about there." I then cut the mobile phone call off. "What's it got to do with you?" I said with what I thought was an unconcerned look. This probably wasn't the right tone to adopt with such an aggressive and muscular man, but I did it anyway. "That was my mate, and you put him in hospital for three weeks," he snarled.

There were two options available to me. Either apologise profusely for any offence or injuries caused or show some hitherto unseen bravado. "I'm going to shoot you lot dead, and that's a promise." Specks of spit were now flying from his mouth. There was a theme developing here with saliva.

If ever there was a reason to say something that perpetuated certain stereotypes, preservation of my life was certainly the best one. "We're Muslims, we welcome death. If you want a holy war, you'll definitely get one," I said with the sternest tone I could muster. I stopped just short of shouting "Allahu Akbar," which would almost certainly have put the fear of God into him. Never mind a war, I wasn't capable of a minor difference of opinion. He then made a gun sign with his fingers and pointed it at me, and declared, "We'll see," before he stormed out. Against all odds, he'd believed the absolute tosh I was talking to sound tough. The sound of blaring police sirens interrupted me mid-sigh of relief. Unbeknownst to me, my brother had called the police, and moments after he left, a swarm of police cars screeched to a halt outside. All the officers were armed and rather worryingly, the officers immediately recognised Tim. They stopped him outside the pub and conducted a search on his person. I could hear one police officer telling the people at the end of the radio that it was a local villain and mentioned his name. They then sent him on his way, and he went back into the pub. The last thing I wanted was to be on the wrong side of some local villains. There was little doubt in my mind it was not the last I would hear of Damian and Tim. One of my staff said he was friends with a local Asian hard case named Yasser, who ran a lot of the doors at nightclubs in the area and might smooth things over if required.

Later that day, I went to see my friend Ryan, who was another local hard man, to see how much he knew of the two characters I'd had the ding-dong with. He was like the Google of the streets and had previously offered to sort out any problems at the shop because he knew almost everyone locally. It was time to call in that favour. According to Ryan, and to my absolute mortification, my two foes were employees of a major Irish travelling crime family in the city. They'd had television documentaries made about them. It wasn't alarm bells that were ringing but more of an air-raid siren, which was almost sufficient to cause me tinnitus. It filled me with icy dread. The gang was suspected of a lot of the murders in the city. What caused these men to resort to a life of criminality? Money, power, and a sense of belonging were traditionally the motives. Or are some people more psychologically predisposed to committing crime? What nonsense am I talking? I couldn't care less if there were a correlation between their parents not putting their school drawings on a fridge and them shooting innocent take-away owners. They could do whatever they wanted to whomever, as long as they didn't do it to me, my staff, or my property. Being beaten to an almost unconscious state by some nobodies was an ignominy that no self-respecting gang member could bear. Ryan warned against appealing to Damian's better nature because he didn't have one. It was like Ryan was reading from a dossier he had compiled for an upcoming television show or court case. Ryan shook his head and recommended I leave town as soon as possible. He advised me never to look back unless it was for any potential hitmen. I needed a workable solution and some reassurance but was given the plot of an old western film instead. My heart plunged towards the pit of my stomach, and a tidal wave of shock reverberated in and around my head. Ryan wasn't impressed at my suggestion of Yasser smoothing things over either and had claimed Damian would laugh at Yasser. My problems were growing exponentially. What weighed in my favour was that a family member of the crime gang had been murdered a few days earlier, and they were all preoccupied with that. After that day, Ryan never returned to the shop, which clearly showed he didn't want any further involvement, and who could blame him? It wasn't as easy to leave as Ryan had suggested because I had to earn a living, but dying wasn't much of a living either.

My new trajectory had sent me hurtling towards a collision course with the type of scum and villainy normally seen in bars in Star Wars films. A retaliatory attack seemed imminent, and in my mind, it was a question of when rather than if. I had to proceed with as much caution as an overweight mouse in a cat sanctuary. It certainly didn't feel befitting that I should go out being shot while delivering a Doner kebab with extra chilli sauce. The sauce being a chilling metaphor for blood. I always wished my death would be heroic, as I saved a child prodigy who would later discover the cure for cancer from a burning building. For this, I would posthumously receive the George

Cross for bravery. Or it could be more dignified, as an old man surrounded by my family as I told them tales of Derring-Do on the battlefield; that was my life. My last words should be something profound or quotable and certainly not, "Please don't shoot, I'm not sure if my underwear is clean aaarrrrgggghhhhh!!" Or something even dumber than that. My fear was that each spicy bad breath could be my last, or my last, in my current physical form anyway. The one silver lining was that because the police had stopped Tim for making the threats, he would now be on their radar if harm came to us. It might make their gang bide their time.

With a sense of impending doom, I considered my options. There was only one thing to do, play my trump card and speak to the taxi driver. A couple of hours later, he sent his top boy to the shop. The top boy spoke with brevity, confidence, and a business-like manner similar to that of the Mr Wolf character from Pulp Fiction. His appearance was something out of Grand Theft Auto. There didn't appear to be a flicker of human feeling on his weathered face. Even his chin had muscles growing out of it. His front gold tooth, chains, earrings, and an 'Angel of Death' tattoo on his arm gave him an air of menace. If ever a man's appearance screamed 'gangster,' it was his. There wasn't any concern on his face when I mentioned who he was dealing with, and he merely said to let him worry about that. He'd never heard of Damian or Tim but knew of their bosses. He gave me his mobile number and assurances he would be only four minutes away if I needed him. When being attacked by violent and deranged men, four minutes was a long time to be waiting. This world of violence and gangsters was something I didn't want to be anywhere near, but I had no choice. I thanked him for his support and prayed I never saw him again.

It was going to be fight or flight, and I'm not ashamed to admit that flight was the best option, as per Ryan's advice. It was better to be a living coward than a dead hero. I only wanted to get out alive and didn't want to end up being another gangland statistic. The staff was all local, and it was best to offer them the shop if it was the quick sale I desperately craved. My dad took some persuading to sell up because he wanted to stay and face the problem head-on, but he eventually relented. The delivery driver offered to take the shop and was perfectly aware of the previous goings on. He mentioned his nephew was heavily involved with a major gang in the city, and the matter would easily be quashed. As I signed the contract to sell the shop, I waved goodbye to the city and all its unsavoury characters as well as all its violent shenanigans. The feeling was more relief than elation.

My swift departure was a bit of an anti-climax. There was still a lingering doubt they would track me down, but thankfully, it never came to fruition. On my last day at the shop, I informed the landlord of the pub to put the word out that the old owners had sold up. Hopefully, word would filter back to Damian, Tim, or whichever ne'er-do-wells had been contracted to facilitate my demise. If they tried to seek me out, they would have been searching for 'Dave' from Leeds because those were the details I had given to everyone. My real forename had been difficult to pronounce for many people, and I had chosen a solid English name for convenience. It's with great shame to admit I was embarrassed to say I was from Bradford, but it may have helped throw people off the scent. Hopefully, they would have moved on with their lives, and carried on with their nefarious pursuits, while I became nothing more than a dimly lit memory for them. Only four days after selling the shop, I was offered my dream job, and I quit the electrical installation course. When people asked me why I sold the shop, I explained that if I had remained there, it would have been injurious to my physical and mental health. Well, I wasn't lying.

A few months after selling the shop, I spoke to the new owner and asked him if there had been any comeback from the Damian incident. His version of events was that a few of Damian's associates had gone into the shop armed with baseball bats, but when they recognised his nephew, they had a few minutes of inconsequential chit-chat and ordered food. Academics in search of proof of violence breeding violence need to look no further than these events. Sometime later, I relayed the story to my friend, and he remarked it was something straight out of a film. I asked if he meant Four Lions because of the "holy war" comment. He chastised me and claimed he meant the British gangster film Lock, Stock, and Two Smoking Barrels.

THE CHAPTER ABOUT HOW I TRY TO BRING CLOSURE TO THE WHOLE DES WALKER SAGA

As time passed, I mellowed towards Des, and the pain from 1999 was virtually forgotten. My story couldn't end with a deeply embarrassing encounter. You could imagine my glee when I discovered that Des was about to do a fan's event in November 2019 in Nottingham. The most expensive ticket purchased a seat at the same table as Des Walker and a meal. This was like music to my hairy ears. By this stage, I felt sufficient time had passed for him not to recognise me from 1999. There wouldn't even be any requirement for the services of a plastic surgeon or an elaborate disguise. If nothing else, the ageing process alone would shield me from any embarrassment. As I took my seat at the table, I felt I was tantalisingly close to fulfilling one of my greatest lifetime ambitions. Would I return home with a fresh wave of euphoria, or would I be as deflated as a weight loss champion? My heart was thumping so loudly, and I could hear it. The sweat on my palms was almost dripping, and I was desperately wiping it on my trousers in case there were any handshakes.

Des Walker then appeared, like a mirage in a desert. Nessun Dorma, the haunting BBC theme tune for the 1990 World Cup, was playing in my head, and I felt like humming it. It was like being transported back to the hot and glorious summer of 1990. My heart swelled scarily inside my chest. People took the other seats at the table while Des signed autographs. By an amazing stroke of luck, the only seat left was next to me. As Des took his seat, he shook my once sweaty hand. He didn't appear to wipe his hand on anything, which suggested I had saved the day on the sweaty palm front. How do I not come across as a blathering idiot? Not a simple task for someone who has a lifelong history of misjudging situations and a mastery of faux pas. You should google this French term because I did after I heard someone use it. It sounded deliciously clever, cultured, and naturally out of place here. Whatever happened, there mustn't be a repeat of 1999. It seemed surreal; I thought I was dreaming when I was sitting in the next seat to Des Walker. If I could have met any living celebrity, it would definitely have been Des Walker, and I told him this. It's difficult to say what he made of such a bold statement, but it got his attention, judging by his raised eyebrows.

At one point, he even joked that I knew more about him than he did, and I think he was right. When I told him he'd inspired me to play football, he nodded his head, and it was like a gesture of solidarity between two kindred spirits. I felt like the little kid in the classic western movie SHANE, who hero-worshipped the fast gun drawing, titular gunfighter. The little kid was also infatuated with speed, just like me. I had always wanted to ask him about the quickest players that he'd played with and against over the all-important short distance. He had no hesitation in naming Franz Carr, a former Nottingham Forest teammate, as the fastest player he ever played with. Nobody was ever going to outrun a Carr, and certainly not a Walker.

The fastest player he had played against was going to be Overmars or Adamczuk, and he went for Overmars. This was a little surprising because it appeared Adamczuk had made up just as much ground on him as Overmars. Had he forgotten about how fast Adamczuk was? "So, it wasn't Adamczuk, then?" I inquired. He gave me a look of genuine confusion and asked, "Who?" He didn't even remember Adamczuk, the man who had literally caused me nightmares and sleepless nights at the same time. It appeared Des wasn't as affected by being outpaced by Adamczuk as I had been by witnessing it. Maybe it was better he'd forgotten about him, and I wish I'd never heard of him. Either that or he hadn't heard me clearly. There were some questions in relation to what had transpired in 1993 I wanted to ask, but he didn't need to be reminded of the worst period in his professional career. This might have been interpreted as being disrespectful.

It would have been interesting to know if he had felt as depressed as I was by being outpaced so easily and how he was affected by being frozen out of the England scene. Apart from the speed business, the other question I wanted an answer to was whether he had any intention of writing an autobiography. The answer was a categoric and comprehensive 'no,' in keeping with his views on privacy. Maybe he can read about my life if I can't read about his.

There was then a break from our conversation, and I tried to take a selfie with him, but he was looking the other way. When he noticed what I was trying to do, he moved closer to me and into view. I'm not a good enough writer to explain in words how this made me feel. The selfie was blurry, as my phone was five years old at the time, and the camera had seen better days. When it was purchased, it was the best one available. It still worked, and I didn't have any intention of replacing it. My policy for my phones, cars, and women is exactly the same. I stay with them until they die on me. Although, my wife and car were never the best ones available. A chicken dinner was then provided, but I did not partake in this. It was due to religious dietary restrictions rather than my incompetence with knives and forks, like a lot of you will be assuming. As we were sitting at the table after the meal, Des was talking to his partner, and I was trying to look busy on my phone because I didn't wish to irritate him unnecessarily. He then gently tapped me on the elbow and inquired if

I was alright. He also asked if I was having a good evening. That was such a nice touch and made me feel elated. When he touched my elbow, it felt like a bolt of lightning. He did have superpowers, after all. It was evident he knew how important the evening was for me. He then took centre stage at the front of the hall and told hilarious tales from his playing days. Des proved to be a charismatic and eloquent orator. The guests were in stitches and even applauded at numerous points.

As I was about to leave, I thanked my hero for a marvellous evening and for fulfilling my boyhood dream. He wished me a safe journey back to Bradford and gave me a manly handshake. The Des Walker story and my sweat had come full circle. As I left, I felt a genuine sense of accomplishment; I had achieved a personal and challenging goal. This was an unprecedented feeling for someone who was the epitome of laziness. As with any lifetime goal that is achieved, it leaves a void. Where there was once a pursuit of Des Walker, there was now emptiness. This journey lasted over thirty years, and it was finally over. My mood was even better than that of a freshly married gold digger or Amy Winehouse's ex-husband's street pharmacist. The reason I have mentioned Winehouse's ex-husband is because I had seen him in a shop once, and he looked like the perfect example to use in this instance. (If you think I'm doing footnotes to explain any references, you're sadly mistaken. We live in the technological age, and Google or Ask Jeeves can help you).

A few months later, I discovered self-publishing and decided to write my life story. My life story wouldn't be complete without the odd mention of Des Walker. What seemed like a great idea at the time was that the story would end with Des Walker being offered the manuscript of this book. This might add some much-needed suspense, I thought. The next event was due to be held in August 2021, and I booked my ticket without any reservation. The event had the option of a seat at the same table as Des Walker, Stan Collymore, or three other players who aren't important enough for me to even name. My book wouldn't be completed until after that meeting, obviously. One of my concerns was whether Des would recognise me (I was confident he would) and what he would make of it. Had he sought an injunction against me since our last meeting? There was nothing to lose, apart from possibly my liberty and self-respect. There was no way to have known how he would react to being offered an envelope with the manuscript of an unpublished book. Would he suspect I was trying to make money from his name, which I wasn't? I wasn't sure if he'd consider it a complete waste of his time or would perhaps even view me as a bit of an oddball. Was he even a reader, would he care?

The idealist in me was confident Des would be elated that he inspired someone enough to feature prominently in a book. The realist in me suspects he will be receptive and respectful but may never actually read it. Every eventuality had gone through my head. My position as a writer was unique in that not even I knew what would happen next. This was exciting, as well as suspenseful, and I'm not saying this to set up a dramatic finale for the ending of the book. There could be epic humiliations, fairy tale endings, or plot twists. There were times it seemed like a preposterous idea, and at other times, it seemed like a masterstroke. Another area of debate in my head was whether to leave my email address at the end of the manuscript for him to contact me with feedback. This seemed too presumptuous, even for me. To gain complete closure, it was decided not to leave any details. I didn't want to be sat waiting for contact from Des. In what was a sign of things to come, the event organisers were running half an hour late, even though they had 18 months to prepare for it. They would be better described as event disorganisers. While I was waiting, I spoke to a couple of other attendees, and I explained why I was there. They were polar opposites physically. One was tall, slim, and with extremely long hair, and this means the other guy was short, overweight, and bald. They would have been a perfect blend for a successful comedy double act if it were the 1940s. I shared my anxieties with them, but they were confident I had nothing to worry about.

The pressure was mounting, and I was questioning myself more than ever. Was this even worth it? Probably not, was my honest assessment. All the old doubts came flooding back, but I had to do it for the book.

The chance of Des sitting next to me was pretty slim, but it didn't really matter because the moment of truth wouldn't happen at the table anyway because I had to catch him alone. He came and sat three seats from me, but as soon as he sat down, the announcer stood on the stage and drowned out any conversation, especially since my table was the closest to the stage. The person sitting next to Des was speaking to him, but even from a few feet away, the context of their conversation was lost on me. The only thing I heard was Des being asked if he still watched football, and he replied he didn't. That made two of us, but I wondered if it was for the same reasons. The players were then called up to the stage. This had given us approximately fifteen minutes with Des at the table. It wasn't Des' fault, but the event organisers would have struggled to organise a heroin purchase in Bradford. It was all frightfully mundane and about as much fun as watching dry paint become flaky.

During the break, I went to use the toilets and saw the long-haired individual, who enquired if I had handed over the manuscript. The look I gave him must have been one of disappointment as I told him I hadn't had the opportunity. His advice was, "You have to do it. Otherwise, you'll be an old man and asking yourself a lot of what-if questions." As I did some deep pyscho-analysis of the situation, I realised it wasn't the fear of being embarrassed that was causing me anxiety. It was more to do with the fear that an unpleasant experience would destroy all the goodwill of the last meeting and my childhood memories. I hadn't spent more than a year writing this book and paid good money for the ticket to simply chicken out at the last minute. The long-haired guy was right. I didn't want to live a life of sorrow and regret. It would also have been cowardly to abort the mission at this late stage, but the fear of failure was agonisingly real.

If the announcer wasn't so loud on his microphone, I would have fallen asleep. I had paid a lot of money to have Des sit at my table, and I'd only received fifteen minutes of loud noise, drowning out conversations with him. Whilst on the stage, Des spoke about how important the fans were to him. That sealed it for me, I was going to hand the manuscript over. As the evening drew to a close, the players got up to leave, apart from Des and Collymore, who were in a deep conversation but looked as though they were about to get up. Des, Collymore, and I were all on the edge of our seats, as I hope you are right now.

My seat was only a few feet from him, and I didn't have to travel very far. I approached Des and asked him if I could have a quick word with him in private. He replied, "Of course," as he graciously walked off the stage and stood next to me. This really was the moment of reckoning, and I had his undivided attention. My peripheral vision detected other fans approaching like vultures to steal my limelight, and I had to be quicker than a Marc Overmars burst. There would only be seconds before we lost this hard-earned and much sought-after privacy. I took a deep, bad breath and composed myself. This was a moment I would remember for the rest of my life. "Would you mind if I took a photo of you for the front cover of a book I've written about how you inspired me as a child?" I asked nervously and rather expectantly. A lot hinged on his reply. "Absolutely," he replied as he looked keenly in my direction.

He then happily posed as I took a photo of him with a better phone than I had last time, but my hand was shaking a little bit. That photo is the one you can see on the front cover of this book. A photo taken by me adds authenticity to the book, and it's what I had always planned. Incidentally, the photo on the front cover of the Asian child, is one of myself from the early 1980s. This was an intense, high-stakes moment. It was too late to think about the consequences.

"This is the manuscript, and I'd like you to read it," I proclaimed as I showed him the envelope. "It would be an honour. I promise to read it, and I'll buy the book too when it's published. My fans mean a lot to me," he said as he took the envelope from my hands with a wide and glowing smile. His eyes appeared to sparkle with merriment. This had exceeded my most optimistic expectations. I was curious if he'd remembered me, and I wasn't talking about 1999. "Don't know if you remember me, but we've met before?" I asked with some confidence. "I do. It was the event a couple of years ago." Why did I ever doubt the great man? We then lost the privacy as fans wanting to speak to him surrounded Des. I had planned to tell him it wasn't a love letter and definitely wasn't a copy of 'Misery,' but time was my enemy. I placed my hand on his shoulder and said goodbye, as I knew I wouldn't get another chance to have a meaningful conversation with him. Everything I wanted to say was in the manuscript, anyway. He looked at me and gave a polite nod. The fan with the long hair then walked past me, and I told him I had done it. He saw Des with the envelope in his hand and congratulated me. He asked what the title of my book was and that he would buy it. Let's hope he keeps his word. This guy and Des could be my only two potential customers. The version I handed to Des Walker had too much football for the average reader, and my editor had advised me to remove a lot of it. The eagle-eyed amongst you might have realised that this is the third edition of the book, and this is because I removed more and more football with each edition. It may surprise you, but I did hire a professional Editor, Book Cover Designer, and Formatter. Sadly, I couldn't afford a Ghost Writer.

The one person whom I hope reads this book, or the manuscript anyway, is Des Walker, unlike the letter I had written to him back in 1999. There's no doubt in my mind he will, because Des Walker is not a man known to mince his words, and I don't have any reason to disbelieve him. This is unless he has some previously unseen acting skills of an Oscar-winning thespian, like Jodie Foster.

If I was to ever see him again, I would ask "Did you read my book?" If he does read it, I can proudly claim that my hero knows more about my life than I know about his. How many people can make that claim?

THE CHAPTER WHERE I TELL YOU WHAT I AM DOING IN 2021

In 2005, I was successful in attaining my dream job. By dream job, I don't mean professional football player because that was never a realistic possibility. I don't mean a job where I could sleep and dream, either. For reasons of security, accountability, and privacy, I'd rather not divulge the exact nature of my work. However, there is an abundance of clues for any half-decent amateur sleuths. You already have some clues, and there are more to follow. This job can only be described as a massive overachievement, but it comes with its own complications. As with a lot of over-achievers, I suffer from "Imposter Syndrome." It had caused me to worry that there was a mistake in Human Resources when they offered me the job, and it would unmask me as the talentless buffoon I am. The only courses I put myself forward for are essential ones, as I have severe concentration and confidence issues.

What might seem simple to my colleagues can be as difficult as trying to climb Mount Everest backwards, equipped only with a walking stick and flip-flops for me. My supervisors have attempted to up-skill me, but their attempts have been thwarted, as I have put up some fierce resistance. Why waste the organisation's time and embarrass myself in the process? That's exactly what Homer Simpson would have done. He's a bit of a role model to me. Not through choice, but something that has been forced upon me. Even refresher courses cause me to worry necessarily (yes, I mean necessarily) because I only scrape by. Why step out of my comfort zone if there isn't any need? Due to this, I will forever remain a foot soldier, but unlike many people, I am fully abreast of all my limitations. This doesn't mean to say that I am incompetent at my job. If my performances are judged purely by my annual appraisals, I am an average performer. For someone who is synonymous with mediocrity, average is an outstanding achievement. Oh, what I'd give to be average at everything. The year of my peak and optimum performance was in 2012, when I was rated an above-average performer. This wasn't an administrative error, as everyone else and I believed. It wasn't a case of mistaken identity either.

My ethnicity isn't ever an issue at work apart from when I'm expected to take in samosas and shami kebabs on my birthday when most others take in Asda doughnuts. Growing up, we never celebrated birthdays because it was a year closer to death. Why would I celebrate some random date when I was born, which reminds me I'm old and nearing death? Birthdays shouldn't be celebrated; we should mourn them. Age might only be a number, but it's still the most accurate method of determining the state of a body and its future lifespan. It's a bit like when people say they saved someone's life. Nobody's life is ever saved because everyone dies in the end. Death is merely delayed.

My job requires me to deal with confrontation on an almost daily basis, and it's something the old me would have really struggled with. It's not an issue for me now, and it's partly due to watching UFC. This doesn't make me some sort of tough guy because I don't think I could ever be that. The fear of being beaten up has totally gone, and it would probably have never been realised if it wasn't for my job. I wish it had happened sooner, but some things aren't meant to be.

The thing I struggled with the most in my job was the driving because I couldn't initially achieve the required level of competence. My inability to drive in my job was similar to not being able to use a screwdriver as an electrician. This meant I had to work harder than others to prove my worth to the organisation at the beginning. After a lot of private training, I passed the test, and I still rank it as my greatest achievement. Just as it took me longer to pass my normal driving test than anyone I'm personally aware of, it also took me longer to pass my work driving test longer than anyone I'm aware of. This possibly set an organisational record, according to the examiner. I put more effort into passing the driving than anything I'd ever done previously or ever will do. It was my personal Mount Everest, or maybe my personal K2. This is the Pakistani mountain that isn't as tall as Mount Everest but believed to be harder to conquer. I'm never going to be a good driver, but I'm not dangerous either. I'll have to settle for being merely adequate and, as with everything else in my life, completely without flair.

My working style is like Des Walker's style of play in that I am happy to perform the thankless and monotonous aspects of my work while the talented people deservedly take the glory. The only time I can make a big noise anywhere is because of flatulence. To those who say I don't lift a finger, I salute you with one finger, and you can guess which one. My only career ambition is still not to get sacked, and I want to be the grey man who goes unnoticed. The only time I would be the best employee would be if everyone else was on strike.

Watching football doesn't interest me now, and I have watched little for almost 20 years. Our relationship is like that of a divorced couple who will never be amicable. Or is that like a married couple? There has simply been too much suffering for any type of reconciliation. The UFC is now my only sporting love, and I consider myself a third Dan black belt in watching it.

It was befitting that I should retire from playing football at roughly the same time as Des Walker. In 2017, some of my friends started to play 5-a-side football and asked me to play. It had almost been twenty years since I'd last played, and I was reluctant because of fear of embarrassing myself. After some intense negotiations, they eventually convinced me to take part because being rubbish at football doesn't bother me much now. The passage of time had made my ball control even worse. Fortunately, even as a middle-aged man, my speed hasn't deserted me entirely. However, my legs won't hold up for anything more than about a single ten-metre sprint.

As homage to Des Walker, I wear a custom-made shirt with the slogan, "YOU'LL NEVER BEAT…" but with my name on it. To be as professional as possible, I wear a full Bradford City kit, but the shirt is occasionally substituted for those with Des Walker-related phrases, so it reminds the opposition of who they're up against.

Something that I have often wondered was whether there was a bigger Des Walker fan out there. I'd love to meet that person and compete to prove my superiority. Nobody has previously written a book about how Des Walker affected their life; therefore, I have surely outdone any potential rivals. I would like to issue an open challenge to any pretenders to my throne because I feel I am the ultimate authority on the subject. If Des ever became a news item, I would be called upon for expert analysis. On the flip side, if I'm honest with myself, I wish I'd never had this fascination with Des Walker. The anguish of 1993 and the years that followed was as great as any football fan has ever had to endure. My love affair with football might not have started with Des Walker, but it definitely finished with him. If it wasn't for Des Walker, I'd still be a big football fan instead of the bitter and twisted ex-fan I ultimately became. Conversely, if it hadn't been for Des, I'd have stopped playing football. I still mourn the lost opportunities of Des Walker's career because it promised so much and ended in underachievement. This is obviously, in complete contrast to my own life, as I have achieved more than I could have imagined.

My health is still good, and my sickness record at work is unblemished. This may have something to do with the fact that I have entirely avoided tobacco, alcohol, and drugs. With the passage of time, my nose has become fuller, and it isn't because of my lies, as my wife believes, but more to do with the ageing process. At 22 and over a three-month period, I lost my hair, and the little hair I had left could easily sit on a coconut without arousing any suspicion. I didn't really lose it entirely; it started growing inwards and sprouted out of my nose and ears. My nasal hair makes both the Amazon rainforest and a bird's nest jealous. It manages to spread faster than a rumour at my wife's weight watchers or anger management meetings.

After 25 years of being bald and having horseshoe-shaped hair at the back of my head, I had Scalp Micro-pigmentation. This means that my hairline has made the biggest comeback since the food of a supermodel at a pre-shoot buffet. The procedure gives the illusion I have a full head of hair but choose to shave it. Thankfully, I am still of slim build, but due to the lockdown, I have put on a bit of extra weight recently, as I had quite a lot on my plate. The wearing of masks during the Covid-19 lockdown has been a blessing because I have saved a small fortune on mints, but there was a price to pay as I had to constantly smell my own breath.

I say lame dad stuff, and my kids tell me that the sole purpose of my existence appears to be to annoy them. Isn't that what all parents do? They exact their vengeance by buying tweezers and waxing kits for me as presents on most Father's Days. One of their latest presents was a mug that read, "World's greatest farter, I mean father." The first part was definitely correct. Just like their mum, my kids haven't shown any interest in reading this book. They might after I pass on, but I'm not convinced.

As I've got older, I'm finding it even tougher to retain information, and my hearing appears to be getting worse. Either that or everyone around me is whispering. Some inconsiderate people have accused me of using this as an excuse to do even less at home and at work. My near sight has deteriorated enough to give the impression that I'm taking a selfie when trying to read something.

Curry is my favourite food now, but I certainly don't have it fourteen times a week. My ethnicity and heritage are not important to me, but I'm certainly not ashamed of it. My dad reckons I should hand in my Asian card. Pakistan is undeserving of my allegiance because Britain has given me opportunities I wouldn't have had otherwise. This country's liberal values mean I can practice my faith without fear of discrimination or any intervention from the state, unlike a lot of countries. Britain is my home, and I consider myself British. Had I expressed this view in the 1980s or '90s, I would have been ridiculed and vilified by my community.

My Islamic faith is the most important thing in my life, and it gives me peace that nothing else could. I appreciate it's not fashionable to express any type of religiosity or belief in a higher power. It could put some people off, but you're getting what I truly believe. It's definitely not blind faith, and I based the decision on reasoning. Having an unflinching faith is akin to knowing the winning lottery numbers. When I've felt down, my faith is the one thing that helped me get through it. My core beliefs are to be good to everyone and to promote harmony, but I accept there are those of my faith who interpret it in a radically different way. There isn't anything anyone can say about my faith that would anger me. No amount of Salman Rushdie-type books or cartoons will ever upset me. My reply to anyone who tries to offend me would be that they have their beliefs, and I have mine. I hope you don't think this is turning into a sermon, so I'll steer it back a little bit.

One constant feature in my life has been that I always wanted to be like other people, but I am finally happy just being me. If I had more about myself or was even average at most things, it could have led to arrogance. My blessings are innumerable and profound, for which I'm eternally grateful. I have lived the English dream. My life has shown that it's fine to be imperfect, fun-loving, and have feeble ambitions. Although reality television, rappers, and Jedward have proven that the lack of talent isn't a barrier to success anymore.

My mortality features prominently in my thoughts now, and I have fully come to terms with it. As a child, when I first became aware of my mortality, I recalled asking God to allow me to live until the age of forty-five. It seemed long enough away at the time for me not to worry, and I felt I'd negotiated a pretty good deal. As I approached the age of forty-five, I wanted to negotiate an extension. Some type of extension appears to have been granted, as I am still here to write the book and just past the age of forty-five. Ultimately, my aim is to die before my children and after my parents. I don't want to become a burden on the state or my family and would prefer to die while I'm still reasonably healthy. This would be preferable to becoming senile and pumped full of drugs or wearing nappies. As I carry my baby grandson in my arms, I hope when I go, he will be big and strong enough to be one of the people to carry my coffin. Whether I achieve this, I may never know. There is absolutely no doubt in my mind that there is an afterlife, so if you read this after my death, don't worry. I'm in a better place. What advice would the me of today have given to the younger me? It would be not to worry about being totally useless at everything because things will work out in the end.

THE CHAPTER WHERE I TELL YOU WHAT SOME OF THE OTHER CHARACTERS FROM THIS BOOK ARE DOING IN 2021

DES WALKER.
All I can tell you about him is that he trains Indonesian boys to play football and does fan's events.

MY DAD.
We have made peace in our own way, but we still haven't had a meaningful conversation though. It's possibly too late now to become best friends and have a father/son relationship that would be considered normal by today's standards. He's now more open-minded than people a lot younger than him and has come a long way for someone who once advocated honour-based violence. He was a product of his environment and upbringing, as most of us probably are. He makes a real effort with his grandkids, and they all love him. I might even translate this book for him, for old time's

sake. The black and white passport photo of the Asian man on the cover is of my dad from the 1960s.

MY WIFE.

She still tries to operate an Orwellian Society in our house, where any uprising or attempted coups are quickly quashed. What little freedom and privacy I have left is taken by Apple, Google, and various rogue governments. The only place I have any freedom is in my head, but I'm waiting for Big Tech to invent something to counter that. Freedom of speech? I don't think so.

MY COUSIN.

He's now an overweight grandad who can still almost do the splits. His hands, arms, and presumably the rest of him are still like granite. He's on his fifth and surely last wife, which proves that persistence overcomes resistance. Unless he's going for some type of modern-day British record, he'll struggle to beat the world record due to the polygamous cultures of certain countries. We have grown apart now and are completely different people.

BIG JIM.

He left Danka to work at, wait for it, a brewery. It later went bust. It would be wrong of me to speculate if it was down to him, but I suspect it was. He saw out the rest of his working life as a Traffic Warden. Sadly, I've not seen him in years, but I don't regularly frequent the all-you-can-eat establishments of Bradford.

KAMRAN.
He now works in a Community Centre in a role that was sold to him as only having to switch on a television for the elderly users. He was up in arms when he discovered he had to also answer the phone and use the photocopier. Trust me, I'm not joking. He correctly predicted that I would be doing all the electrical work at his house for free.

SHAHID.
As you've probably established already from his aggressive and unhelpful nature, he now works for the civil service in a call centre. The man must take his work seriously, as he doesn't answer his personal phone either. When he started there in 2006, people were taking bets on how many weeks he would last. He has put enough weight on now for him never to be described as skeleton staff.

THE BUSINESS STUDIES GRADUATE WHO CLAIMED HE WOULD ONLY BE A DANKA FOR A FEW WEEKS.
He's still there in 2021 after 23 years, but in a different department and working very hard. He is still awaiting something better. That's a perfect illustration of why life is so unfair.

THE SMALL BULLY.

(The one I avenged) Saw him in July 2021, and I offered him a lift. I explained I was writing a book about my life and that he got a mention. He wouldn't stop apologising for the bullying and appeared to be genuinely remorseful. I told him it was 35 years ago and to forget it ever happened. It was unsurprising when he told me he had also been bullied by the big bully.

THE BIG BULLY. (The one I didn't avenge)

I saw him a couple of years ago in a park. He looked dangerously overweight and was sitting on an undersized bench, which was struggling to contain his girthy backside. He was almost as bald as I was but was fighting it more than he did with his obesity. His hair made a crescent shape around the back of his head, but he still had a fade on the edges. The strangest thing about his hair was the comb-over, which looked as though he had glued some thin laces on one side of his head in a valiant but fruitless attempt to cover his scalp. He had two teardrop tattoos under one of his eyes. In urban mythology, each tear represents a person they've killed. Or did it represent his crimes against fashion? He was using his stomach as a table for his family-size deep pan pizza. Stood next to him was a large bottle of Diet Coke, which in his mind, probably made it a healthy meal. If I were to see him again, I would kill him with kindness by buying him a Doner kebab. Not any old Doner, though. It would be the biggest, most calorific, trans-fat, and salt-laden one available. This is what he would have really wanted, instead of a 5k charity walk in his memory in a couple of years or having a plaque with his name being placed on that bench. I hope he doesn't read this. He won't unless I have one of my famous brainwaves and publish this book on the inside of 24-inch pizza boxes. I suspect he has an abundance of life coaches, support workers and more therapists than the entire UK population had in 1921.

GEORGE LAYTON.

George is practically retired now but has been active on Twitter about his lockdown activities. Later this year, he is doing a fan's event in London. That's too far to travel, and I'll have to wait for him to do an event more local to me. He's in his late 70s now but still in good health. George could be the subject of my second book. Operation George Layton may commence now that Operation Des Walker has reached a satisfactory conclusion.

ANDY LAPTEW.

Passed away in 2019 of cancer, but he had a reasonable amount of screen time in the Netflix documentary series named 'Ripper,' which was broadcast shortly after Sutcliffe's death in December 2020.

SONIA SUTCLIFFE.

She's probably plotting revenge through legal action

against Steve and possibly me. Hopefully, it's Steve she's really after. Actually, I would welcome any legal action from Sonia, as it would generate the type of publicity to make my book a bestseller. If I was Steve, I'd offer her the £30 back.

STEVE.

As stated earlier, Steve is now an extremely busy self-employed electrician. He was suitably worried about Sonia to claim if she ever made contact, he'd tell her he'd moved to a nondescript fishing village on the South coast. My advice to him would be to move to a country that doesn't have an extradition treaty with the UK. I've never met anyone who has a greater love for Asian food than Steve, and he claimed he would have happily swapped places with me in the 1980s if it meant he would have curry fourteen times a week. In early 2021, he developed an unhealthy obsession with Parathas. For those not versed in Asian cuisine, they are greased chapattis. At his most addictive, he had twenty per week but has now got it down to five. He refuses to seek professional help about it and claims it's something he has to simply live with.

What you read above was written in 2021, but there were some significant developments regarding Steve in 2022. One of the biggest regrets of my life had been that I had failed to complete the Electrical Installation course and hadn't learned much of the practical side of it either. I knew enough to never call an electrician to my house, but I felt it was a loose end I simply had to tie up. It was something I wanted to do for a living when I retired from my current job. Steve agreed to take me on as his dogsbody and teach me the practical side on my days off from my normal job. To achieve the qualifications, I could do a fast-track course. On the third day of working together, Steve stated he wanted to finish early as it was a Saturday, and he wanted to go and watch Bradford City play football. I was due to go on a holiday a few days later for a couple of weeks, and we agreed on the date of our next working day as we parted company.

Two days later, I received a text message from Dan stating that Steve had possibly died in bed at some point over the weekend. Steve didn't have any health problems that I knew of, and it made the whole thing difficult to digest. Dan claimed someone named John had gotten the message to him. I asked him if this John person might have got our mate Steve mixed up with another Steve. Dan assured me that even though John was about 75 years old, he certainly wasn't senile. Apparently, Steve's girlfriend had told someone called Lee, who told Abigail, who told John, who told Darren to get the message to Dan. I'd received this information 7th hand and only knew Dan from the chain of narration. Dan lived in Keighley and was dealing with the death of his father-in-law, so he wasn't in a position to start making enquiries. Not even Dan was certain that the information he'd given me was totally reliable.

One way to find out was to call Steve's mobile phone, but it simply rang out. This wasn't unusual because of the nature of his work. One thing about Steve was that if I ever sent him a text message requesting that he should contact me urgently, he always did. When he didn't reply for an agonising half an hour, I became very concerned. The fear of not knowing for sure was making me very anxious, and I decided to finish work early to go to Steve's mum's house. It was a difficult drive, and the closer I got to the address, the more amplified my fears became. When I saw Steve's mum in tears, I knew. Steve was only 44 years old and an only child, but without any children of his own. All this added to his mum's grief. She held my hand and stroked it as a mum would do to a poorly child. Steve had passed away the day before and only 25 hours after we had worked together. On the day of his death, he'd fallen asleep on the sofa in the afternoon at his girlfriend's house, and never woke up. Even though I had seen death many times in my work, this was all so hard to fathom. Myself and Steve's mum spoke about how happy Steve was in our last meeting and how much he was looking forward to getting fitter. He also spoke about the family meal he had planned for that evening. He'd been singing and dancing all the way during our time together that day.

Steve's mum offered to give me all his tools as they were of no use to her. It was something I didn't want to think about because it felt like I would be benefitting from my friend's death. As a mark of respect to Steve, I went and bought his mum her favourite curry from their favourite restaurant, as she hadn't eaten since she'd received the news.

I was out of the country when the funeral took place, but I hope to carry on Steve's legacy by becoming a qualified electrician. It later transpired that the cause of his death was pneumonia, and I'm glad it wasn't the parathas. Since his death, he's appeared in my dreams four times and counting. It could take a while before the dreams stop. In the first dream, I told him he'd passed away, but he assured me he hadn't, and it was all a mistake. On the other occasions, I told him I loved him and missed him. This is something I would never have done while he was alive and well. I like to think he knew how much he meant to me and how much I appreciated him.

When I was going through my own troubles, he would give me his pearls of wisdom, which would put things in perspective. He was the reason I didn't quit the electrical installation course after a few weeks. If I had quit that early, my confidence might have taken an irreversible hit. When I was struggling with the driving at my work, and all my colleagues were passing with ease, he reminded me never to compare myself to other people. His advice helped me to stay optimistic. When I reminded him of those incidents recently, he couldn't recall them and asked in all seriousness if I had him mixed up with someone else. Steve had read the first two versions of this book, and unsurprisingly, the chapter he featured in was his favourite. He actually read that chapter again, about a month before he died, because he loved all the "gangster stuff." The next time it's Eid (the Muslim version of Christmas), I will get emotional because Steve always came to my house for food.

I dedicate this book to Stephen Michael Glot (26/11/77 – 31/07/22), a good electrician, but a better friend. He even shared his birthday with Des Walker. If it isn't obvious to you already, it is Steve on the cover in the workman's gear. May he rest in peace.

My new electrical mentor is a 64-year-old overweight diabetic who has been a chain smoker his entire adult life. He doesn't do any exercise and eats curry every single day. Let's hope our working relationship lasts. If I do make it as an electrician, I'd like to name my company, "Down to Earth Electrical Services", to go with my silly puns and laid-back nature.

RAY HONEYFORD.
His views on integration resurfaced in the media after the Bradford riots of 1995 and 2001 when many prominent social and political commentators claimed he was right all along. He never worked again after he left Drummond and died in 2012.

DAMIAN.
He's probably on painkillers and is suffering from migraines. An internet search many years later revealed

that someone with his uncommon name and from his city had been imprisoned for drug offences. It didn't show a photograph, so I cannot be certain it was him, but it sounds suspiciously like the sort of thing he would do. Despite my best efforts, I'd failed to knock some sense into him. Well, what else did you expect? He was never going to achieve global fame and acclaim for his philanthropic endeavours.

TIM.

He suffered the same fate as his mate and was imprisoned for possessing firearms. A photo confirmed it was him. It suggests the threat to shoot me wasn't an idle one, and I dodged a hail of literal bullets. If and when he is released, I hope he receives twenty phone calls a day from people enquiring if he has had an accident recently. Hopefully, they're all spread out over the course of the day and from different numbers. Not to mention emails and text messages from wealthy men in impoverished countries, with English sounding names, who wish to give him all their riches in exchange for small admin fees. Before I forget, may he also have 20 takeaway leaflets posted through his letter box on a twice-daily basis.

THE TAXI DRIVER.

He is now retired, and his primary pastime is Pakistani politics. He campaigns tirelessly on various social media platforms to bring corrupt politicians to justice. I would imagine it is with the same passion and vigour as he tried to bring fare dodgers to justice.

TOP BOY.
This is a wild stab or a shot in the dark (two things he was certainly well versed in), but I suspect he is either in prison or had made contact with an actual angel of death and not just the one tattooed on his arm.

THE BOUNTY HUNTER.
Miraculously, he's still alive but is beset with health problems. He's still a chain smoker, which hasn't helped. In 2021, there isn't much need for his particular brand of bounty hunting, as forced marriages are virtually unheard of in Britain.

THE POST ROOM.
The internet, and specifically e-mails, have killed the post room. The internet pretty much struck the post room to the top of the head with a heavy metal rolling pin. It was only a matter of time. We all expected a time and motion study to kill it rather than the internet, though. Most of the staff were moved onto real jobs elsewhere.

THE METAL ROLLING PIN.
My brother disposed of it in the industrial bin of a remote Chinese restaurant not long after the incident. He claimed he didn't want it to be traced, and when I suggested his method of disposing evidence was

preposterous, he questioned whether I had wanted to retain it as a grizzly memento. I had a lot of love and affection for it. My hope is that it's giving other people as much pleasure as it did to me, and it's been recycled as a part on a smart electronic device.

BRADFORD.

Whatever became of Bradford? While it isn't some sort of utopia, it's certainly moved on. The driving is still terrible, and it seems like an unwinnable war for the authorities. Why do I still live in Bradford and defend it at almost every opportunity? Because it's my hometown. All my friends and family are here. You could compare it to a long-term loveless marriage that isn't worth ending because of the upheaval it would cause. Bradford is where I've always lived and where, on the balance of probability, I will die. If it is in Bradford that I actually die, I've compiled a list of how it might happen. This is in reverse order of probability.

7) I accidentally electrocute myself.

6) I am killed in a botched robbery at some traffic lights, by a homeless heroin addict, for 50p and a mouldy half-eaten samosa.

5) I am tortured to death by a particularly sadistic serial killer, who was inspired by Peter Sutcliffe and Stephen Griffiths.

4) I am struck in the head with multiple metal rolling pins at the same time.

3) My wife works out that I'm worth more to her in death, than I am alive.

2) I die a natural death.

1) I am mowed down by a dangerous driver at ninety miles per hour in a thirty miles per hour zone, who had gone through two red lights, and had overtaken four cars on the wrong side of the road. He would only have thirty-nine previous convictions for driving and drugs offences, but would be portrayed in the media as a model citizen who was an aspiring architect and a carer for his parents. His elderly neighbour would give interviews to say he had helped her cross the road once and prayed every night for world peace.

Well, what an absolute waste of time that was, but I did warn you. You've lost the most valuable commodity of all, your time, which you'll never get back. This book, much like the cult film, *The Big Lebowski*, has a plot that doesn't make any sense. That's where the similarities end, because the film had a memorable and quotable main character.

Before I go, I'd like to leave you with this final bit of advice, if you, or someone you know, have been affected by any of the issues raised in this book, the following organisations may be able to help.
notthesamaritans@yahoo.com
www.griefcounsellors4snowflakes.gov.uk
www.tellsomeonewhocares.com

If they can't help, you can always contact me on shafeeqyoussaf@yahoo.com to tell me how rubbish my book was, if it might make you feel any better. If I don't respond to you, it's either because I've forgotten my email password, I've died or I've somehow fallen victim to cancel culture.

Printed in Great Britain
by Amazon

16209989R00081